Acclaim for
Reinvent Yourself: Essential Tools from a Brooklyn Psychiatrist Who Has Seen It All

"With the keen mind of a top-rated psychiatrist, the warm heart of a man who has experienced hardship and pain, and the wit and humor of a comedic performer, Dr. Lops offers his readers a guide to reinventing their lives. Written in a style that simultaneously motivates and informs, his book is destined to become a classic that will be read and referenced for generations to come."
- *Paul Hokemeyer, JD, PhD, Fox News analyst and panelist on The Dr. Oz Show*

"Dr. Lops gives much in this engaging and articulate book—he looks at many interesting and crucial events in his life and distills from them learning points and guidance we can all practice to improve and enrich us. His experiences and counsel about accepting new and diverse opportunities in our lives are gems that can meaningfully broaden one's growth."
- *Richard Pleak, MD, child and adolescent psychiatrist*

"In a culture that has no shortage of self-help reads, here comes a book that offers a fresh and inventive approach to the genre. Mixing genuine and heartfelt reflections on one's own flaws and mishaps as a way of drawing instructive observations and suggestions, Dr. Lops invites his readers to a journey of rediscovering and reinventing their lives. Written in an engaging style that is both playful and didactic, this book will simultaneously counsel and motivate readers."

- *Iliyan Ivanov, MD, Associate Professor, Icahn School of Medicine at Mount Sinai, New York*

"Dr. Lops has written a wonderful autobiographical book chock full of insights and observations. He presents these in a wonderfully entertaining, anecdotal set of stories that reveal a great deal about how we can improve our lives and see the world in a more positive light. His style is funny and entertaining, all the while making salient and perceptive comments about different ways of interpreting events. A thoroughly enjoyable and most informative read from an expert in the field of psychiatry, despite his young age."

- *Alan Hilfer, PhD, Chief Psychologist, Maimonides Medical Center*

REINVENT YOURSELF

ESSENTIAL TOOLS FROM A BROOKLYN PSYCHIATRIST WHO HAS SEEN IT ALL

BY DR. JOHNNY LOPS

TAILWINDS PRESS

Copyright © 2015 by Johnny Lops
All rights reserved. Except as permitted under the U.S. Copyright Act of 1976, no part of this publication may be reproduced, distributed, or transmitted in any form or by any means, or stored in a database or retrieval system, without the written permission of the publisher.

Tailwinds Press
P.O. Box 2283, Radio City Station
New York, NY 10101-2283
www.tailwindspress.com

Published in the United States of America
ISBN: 978-0-9904546-0-1
1st ed. May 2015

Contents

Introduction		1
1	Getting into the Race	7
2	Your Thoughts—Not Always Your Best Friend	21
3	Don't Have Anything Good to Say? Don't Say It at All	37
4	That Ego Has Got to Go	53
5	I Am so Mad: Dealing with Emotions	67
6	Are You Up or Down After a Night with Your Friends?	83
7	No More Victim Mentality: You Can Do It	97
8	Curious like a Cat	119
9	Let's Go! You're Gonna Be Late	135
10	The Power of Humility and Great Mentors	151
11	What Did You Say: The Power of Active Listening	167
12	Home to My Dad: Kill 'Em with Kindness	183
Afterword		199

For my parents, Michael and Eileen
For Maureen
And for the people of Brooklyn, who have shaped my life

REINVENT YOURSELF

INTRODUCTION

I am a boy from Brooklyn. As the title of this book states, I have seen a lot in my short years on this planet. Sheesh, by age 13, I had experienced being shot at and robbed at knifepoint. Someone once tried to blow me up.

I have gradually grown to understand how life circumstances impact our mental well-being and feelings about ourselves.

In the fall semester of my senior year in college away from Brooklyn, my roommate and I hunted for an easier class in between our biochemistry and mathematics courses. We stumbled upon a class labeled "Men's Issues." As long as it did not include more equations or atomic structures, we thought it looked like a promising break from all the academic rigor. A class about men and our issues seemed right up our alley.

On day one, I was pleasantly surprised to discover that the class was taught by a woman in her mid-to-late forties. We sat boardroom style; the majority of our classmates seemed to be members of the same fraternity. The class, which focused on thought-provoking and serious topics including dating and sexuality, was also a magnet for immature frat-boy humor and insecurity. Nonetheless, our teacher intrigued me.

You must understand that before this point in my life, I had never even heard of "therapy." I did not know anyone personally who openly told me that he had ever seen a therapist before. One day after class, I summoned up my courage and, like a nerd, clumsily asked if she would mind if, maybe sometime like after school, I could chat with her.

She smiled and replied, "Yes."

We set up a time for me to come to her home the next Friday afternoon. When I arrived, I was surprised to see a home that reminded me of a Victorian cottage out of a Dickens novel, a far cry from a Brooklyn home with its stoops and brick. We sat pleasantly and drank tea out of fine china.

She never called it therapy. Looking back, I am not even sure what degree she had. All I know is that she was an extremely pleasant, easygoing person who welcomed me with an open ear, some warm tea on Friday afternoons, and the chance to vent freely about some of my internal struggles—quite different from my peers from the streets who called me derogatory names for trying to express my emotions and told me to suck it up and *be a man.*

I guess you could say that once a week I went to therapy.

INTRODUCTION

For the rest of the semester, I looked forward to Friday afternoons with excitement. She challenged my assumptions and attempted to guide me towards looking at the life stretching way out ahead of me from other angles and perspectives. She identified the negativity in my life and praised my good self. She encouraged and inspired me to set forth and be the very best me I possibly could be.

Looking back, what mattered most in my meetings with this mentor at age twenty was receiving feedback, guidance, and understanding. It made a difference to receive this support from someone who was grounded, had seen the world, and who could provide healthy nonjudgmental comments with an understanding of where I came from and where I was going.

Sixteen years later and with a lot of experiences under my belt, I now spend my days as a psychiatrist evaluating folks who, like myself back then in 1999, are looking for support and guidance in their journey.

However, as I complete my fourth year after graduation from medical training, understanding the art of psychotherapy and the actual reality of the pressures involved in the practice of psychiatry are two very different ideals. I envision a world where therapy would be provided weekly for all my clients looking into their internal struggles. It would aid and support them in working through their emotional difficulties.

In reality, for many adults and even children (whose cases are typically more complex), many psychiatrists in the community have barely fifteen minutes to provide good work to their clients. It's not their fault, or a result of a lack of training. The reality for many psychiatrists is a caseload of twenty to twenty-five clients daily.

Consequently, on the client side of the equation, the norm has become appointments filled with quick, to-the-point questions about specific psychiatric symptoms. They walk out of the office minutes later with a prescription for a medication. There is no time for them to learn what it is about their psychology, and possibly their social lives, that could have played a role in their symptoms and concerns.

I think back to my kindly teacher during that Men's Issues class back in 1999. If she had instead been a psychiatrist who simply prescribed a medication to me for some of the lows I was experiencing at the time, would I have learned what gradually unfolded about myself during our weekly meetings? I probably would not have developed my personal character traits of resiliency and improved tolerance for dealing with frustration. Those traits have helped me over the years, and I am sure they will continue to help me during many difficult times still to come.

I wrote this book as a way to begin the journey of learning from my experiences to reflect on you and your experiences. You will read a variety of stories from my life.

INTRODUCTION

Some are a little outrageous; all include life lessons. They also include detailed tools and skills I have learned through my continued reflection on my own life, and the observation of my patients' lives, in the hope of inspiring and motivating you. These tools are not based on any specific academic course I have taken in my career, but an accumulation of learning from client encounters and lectures. Over time, I have come to accept that these tools, tailored to the personal psychology of each client, have made my clients' lives easier and more successful.

Take your time reading each chapter. Allow yourself to reread it if you need to, and practice the skills a few times before moving on to the next skill.

As a psychiatrist, providing intimate, personal stories and sharing myself with readers may be unusual. But it doesn't concern me a bit. Alas, I am no longer the person described in many of these stories. My growth and maturity thus allow me to feel comfortable sharing them so that you will come to understand how my hardships—big and small, emotional and external—did not deter me in my quest to achieve success in life. In fact, they only enhanced my ability to face the world.

As with the teacher of my Men's Issues class, let me become your teacher and your mentor as you read this book and absorb the wisdom contained within. Try to relax as you read about my journey and the skills and steps presented. Allow yourself to consider your own experiences through these pages. Think about where you have been, and be open to work on where you are going next.

I hope that you become the best you for today, in the present.

CHAPTER ONE

GETTING INTO THE RACE

"I friggin' hate running. What mile is this? Two? Ugh, I wonder if Maureen would be upset if I just stopped here? Wait. This is exactly what my body wants me to do. It wants me to quit and relax. This is it. It's exactly like life. Mile two of this stupid race is what happens in life when we feel defeated and in pain. Nope. We're gonna keep going. In an hour it will probably be over. I heard there are bagels! Oh yeah, look at that. North part of Central Park is really nice in the spring."

In early 2011, my wife, who is one heck of a runner, encouraged me to take up running. I had completed one race before and had been so happy when it was over. To start running as a serious hobby, with training and a set of goals to achieve, had never been important to me. Don't get me wrong, I have always been athletically inclined and throughout my life have thoroughly enjoyed the competition of basketball. However, basketball is about winning. The most running we did was sprinting down a court—the type of running that I preferred, being relatively speedy.

Thinking about the burden of running by myself, alone with my thoughts as my steps silently hit the pavement, never clicked for me. Running entailed no trash talking, no male bonding, and no delusions of grandeur of one day waking up and dominating the court like Michael Jordan or LeBron James.

At the end of the day, however, I wanted to do something with Maureen. A challenge we could take on together to get inspired. She signed me up for a six-mile race on April 7, 2011. I trained minimally so that I could see, from my day-to-day conditioning, what the experience would be like.

By mile two, I wanted out. "Oh my God, this is torture." My brain hurt. It hurt that the finish line seemed so far away and I was already so bored! I felt every thought in my mind like a weight dragging me down. I wanted to stop running so bad! There was the pressure to not be that guy who quits in the middle. I could not fathom running another fifty minutes. I honestly was cursing myself out for agreeing to do it in the first place. From my vantage point, there was no purpose to this or any understanding of how this could possibly be enjoyable.

I was so wrong. Dead wrong.

When I finished the race on that cold, early April day, so many of life's mysteries began swarming in my head, presumably in the same way Stephen Hawking thinks about black holes. At every session with my clients, I give them challenges. Those challenges can be daunting. My expectation is for them to improve, but on many occasions they resist change. I actually can see my clients' ambivalence when I bark out instructions. Now, more than ever, I understood their bind. *Running for the first time was the accumulation of finally understanding what it was like on the other side of the couch.*

At times in my training, I would have doubts about whether I would continue. Like my clients, I made early mistakes. I signed up for the Brooklyn Half, a half marathon in late May, only seven weeks after my first race. I was so sure that I could use my prior athletic skill to overcome the six-mile race that 13.1 miles seemed to be entirely doable. I began training, but I was a rookie and did not understand the fundamentals: if you are going to train for half marathons, you have to be focused and disciplined. In early May, while engaging in a weekly basketball game, I went up for a rebound and came down on an opposing player's foot. I heard the snap. Two hours later and my foot looked like an elephant's foot! It was awful and I was on crutches until June. It was not my time for a half marathon yet.

My ego got the best of me when I assumed that running was just that, running. But it's not. It takes slow and steady progress. Half marathons are a considerable distance. I rushed trying to accomplish this goal, just as clients try to rush their treatment. I was humbled.

By late June, I was back at it. No more basketball for me. New running shoes and all, I found the ideal place for my nightly runs and I was off. My executive functioning skills were activated. Each upcoming week, I strategized which evenings I could run. I mapped out my days, providing enough time and sacrificing other things on my calendar to complete my runs. If I left work at 7:00pm, I could be home by 7:30pm and still have enough summer evening sunlight until 8:30pm or so. On weekends, setting the alarm to 7:00am allowed a good six- to eight-mile run before the summer daytime heat became a burden.

Week after week, it became easier. Adding an extra mile to my long run every week or two provided a nice comfortable gain to appreciate my newly obtained goals. It reminded me again of therapy, identifying one tool and working a little on it each week, and recognizing how it comes just a tad easier every time. Soon enough, I began not even feeling my legs during the run. I reached a point where my legs felt programmed, my mind afloat as I worked through my thoughts. Running became a place to plan my weeks, work through difficult cases at the hospital, and reflect more about my place in the world. Furthermore, because I was invested, I slept better. Because I was more relaxed, and diet is a vital component of running, I ate better. I pulled back from alcohol intake. My lifestyle changes created a healthier me. Running itself became the most intense antidepressant, anti-anxiety medication, and stimulant I was putting into my body.

Prioritizing my life around work, my relationships, and running, I gradually minimized the negative thoughts in my life. There was no room for them anymore! So what if someone did not call me back or something at work frustrated me? Running became the place to allow those thoughts to float away and prevent them from becoming stronger. It also became my space to modify any thinking around feeling victimized or devalued. I ran, and each time I did, I got better. That was all the validation I needed.

Life became easier. The mundane distractions became less important. I began looking forward to my next race. The day of a run brought an intense enthusiasm. In the moments before the starting gun, I felt like a boxer about to enter the ring to do battle with intense focus and determination. I anticipated that the race would hurt—that there would be pain, and moments of wanting to give up, but my resilience would overcome all. Each race felt like an adventure. My body loved being outdoors, as if I was on the hunt chasing something. The object of the hunt? The finish line.

Aware of the life changes I was making by summer's end 2011, my wife pointed out to me that if I completed nine races, I would automatically qualify for the New York City Marathon. Silence. *I just began running regularly five months ago. Now she is talking about completing 26.2 miles a year from now? Oh yeah we are!*

My curiosity about beginning the journey to become a marathon runner was set. I rested the winter of 2012 and into 2013, and started running again in March 2013.

My first goal was the Brooklyn Half Marathon, the race that eluded me the year before. I found a program online to train for the run and stuck to the regimen. No more basketball this time around. I completed three races prior to the half marathon to regain my momentum to run for time, remembering the necessity of reserving weekends for my training and focusing on adopting a healthier diet and exercise. May 18 came and off we went. The goal was 13.1 miles. I remember experiencing left foot pain before the race started. I diligently tried to ignore it, the same way I tell my clients to ignore their anxious thoughts. I chose to think about what I wanted: to see my parents at the finish line at Coney Island where they would be waiting for me.

"On your mark, go," said the announcer, and off I ran. Four miles into the race, my foot was already hurting. Trying hard to stay focused, my mind already went to arguing that running nine more miles seemed ridiculous. I used all my mental reserve to keep going. Hitting mile six, it was straight through Brooklyn to the end. As I ached running down Ocean Parkway, men dressed like film characters such as the Blues Brothers were passing me with giant smiles on their faces. Then, to make me feel even worse, a man and his dog running together breezed by me at mile eight. By mile ten, something happened. The pain and the anxiety realized they would not win that day. A new natural high, a volt of intense anti-anxiety and anti-pain relief, overcame me, and I felt like I was floating. I increased my speed, sprinting toward the finish line. We turned right onto Surf Avenue entering Coney Island. Up the boardwalk we went, and to the right before the finish line, there were my parents as promised. Giant hugs were shared and I ran to the finish line. My first half marathon was finally complete, but not without its consequences.

By finishing my first half, I felt that completing the journey of the full 26.2 mile marathon had to be done. Early training began July 1.

There was a slight problem. My left foot, already hurting prior to the half marathon, was now in great pain, with a sharp sensation on the top of my foot that ached when running. I went around to physical therapists seeking evaluations. The information was not good. My ankles, knees, and hips were all out of whack. I was not stretching properly and my body created odd, painful compensations for various weaknesses. I was told I needed physical therapy three times a week, but that would not fit into my schedule. What next? I "Youtubed" every physical therapy video I could find for running and bought all the equipment for home use. That's what I call adapting and strategizing!

By August 1, things were coming along, but four weeks had passed from when I was supposed to begin training for the marathon. I told myself that if I was not running by August 7, the marathon was off. Amazingly, with one pain left that was not remitting, I asked a question. I asked a massage therapist about the odd pain on the top of my left foot that still was not resolved.

"Oh," she said. "Just take your foot and stretch it like this." Unbelievable! Three days of this stretching routine and the pain was gone. By August 7, I was out training in high gear again. In four weeks, I kicked up my mileage to an easy ten miles a day. In early September, Maureen and I took a short weekend trip to Chicago and I completed the Chicago Half Marathon. Pretty easy. Four weeks later, it was off to the Staten Island Half Marathon. Done in my fastest time. We were four weeks away from the New York City Marathon and I was scared. Yeah, I had three half marathons in my pocket, but doubling that seemed impossible. As we neared marathon day, I did my twenty-mile training run. Wow, it was intense. By mile seventeen, I was in so much pain. That's when my wife taught me about the wall.

The wall is the moment a runner hits when his body says, *We are done and that's that.* Every step seems just that much more impossible. On this practice twenty miler, I hit my wall at mile seventeen, but I still was three miles away from home. It took another hour just to get home, and that was while shedding intense tears of pain to get there.

Training was coming to an end. The so-called fun part was arriving. Friends began asking where they could watch us. Maureen and I made T-shirts with our names so fans could yell out our names while supporting this inhuman endeavor.

November 2, 2013. I dreaded this day for a long time. On the other hand, I was proud of myself for how crazy this seemed. Eighteen months ago, I barely made it six miles while using every ounce of effort to make it through that race. I had done it. Without even getting through the marathon, I felt proud of myself. I trained hard. I worked through and emerged victorious over the injuries. I continued believing in what I was capable of if I rid myself of negativity, the discouraging words of the friends who asked if I would give up, the distractions, and even my own mind.

The alarm went off and there was no turning back. The amount of work just to get to the starting line was ridiculous! We had to take the subway, then take another train down to Lower Manhattan, then walk, and then head to the Staten Island Ferry. Finally, we had to wait quite a while before getting on the ferry, getting to Staten Island, and waiting in line for a bus. Twenty minutes later, we boarded the bus. It drove us to the foot of the Verrazano Bridge, the starting line.

I had probably driven over the Verrazano Bridge a million times. This time it was weird standing on the Staten Island side, looking towards Brooklyn. From a pedestrian's point of view, I had the privilege of seeing how amazing the bridge actually is—an engineering marvel. I looked up in awe at the size and complexity of the project. A bunch of humans like you and me thought of creating something so magnificent and then actually took products like steel and built it! Aren't humans incredible?

It was time for the national anthem. I almost got teary as the anthem was playing, overcome with joy that I was actually running the New York City Marathon. The gun fired. It began. Up the Verrazano Bridge, I paced myself to avoid expending too much energy as other runners passed me by. Not trying to compete with Maureen's time, I'd already kissed my wife as she went off ahead of me. As we came off the bridge, Bay Ridge was the first part of Brooklyn we ran through. Feeling good. Heading down Fourth Avenue, the crowds were picking up. Having my name "Johnny" emblazoned on my shirt personalized the experience. Each member of the crowd yelled, "Go Johnny. You can do it!"

I reflected on our paths and the necessity of having positive people in our lives. Having two or three people close to us who always say, "Go Johnny. You can do it," in moments of difficulty is so important to our overall mental health. No one in the crowd was playing skeptic and saying, "Who'd ever want to run a marathon? That sounds like a waste of time. So anyway, let me tell you about my tough day." No negativity.

Leaving Fourth Avenue and heading into mile eight, all felt great. There were bands playing, little kids slapping high-fives, and overall I had a big smile on my face. I passed through Williamsburg where I live, saw my parents and gave them a big hug. When did they see Maureen? I asked, feeling a little bit competitive. Was she close? My dad laughed and told me that she'd passed by about thirty minutes ago. Okay, a blow to my ego, but this was my journey of survival, not of competition with the true runner in our family.

As we entered Queens, I knew the wretched Queensborough Bridge was nearing. I'd heard that this marked the first place where many runners hit the wall. I began my ascent up the bridge. It seemed so steep! I raised the volume on my iPod and tried to focus on the bass of the songs I was listening to, trying to let the music guide me. For those readers who have never run long distances before, one of the more interesting subtleties of the human body as a runner is how your stomach tolerates running. Early in my training, I had to adjust what I ate, and when I ate before a run on certain days it felt like I was going to go in my pants right after running. The extent of the gastrointestinal distress—"GI distress"—that I and many runners experience is truly awful.

Continuing on the bridge, I checked in with myself and felt no distress. But what I saw next was shocking and sad. I happened to glance left while on the bridge looking into Manhattan. On the side of the road the GI distress nabbed its next victim. There was a poor woman squatting and having a bowel movement right on the bridge. I couldn't even imagine it. Poor thing. But, as they say, "You gotta do what you gotta do!"

Off the bridge and onto First Avenue, I still felt okay. I still remembered my smile, making eye contact with as many crowd members as I could as I tried to enjoy the experience. We continued up First Avenue, and by mile eighteen, my leg had a new sensation. The old right leg was tightening up a bit. I made my first mental mistake. I was inexperienced and I felt lost on this run, not knowing the future path. I became worried in my head about any more hills and bridges and began panicking about my leg worsening as I hit mile twenty. Again, it reminded me of clients becoming unsettled as they looked too far ahead, worrying about tomorrow when it wasn't here yet. I became agitated that we were still heading up on First Avenue when I knew the finish line was back south.

Then my version of the wall happened. My right leg just stopped bending. I learned later that I had developed ilio-tibio band syndrome, where the muscles in your leg become so tight that it prevents you from bending the entire leg. That meant I had six miles of limping off my right leg. The pain was immense. Felt like a ten out of ten on whatever scale you want to use to measure pain. We were now in the Bronx and heading back down into Manhattan. Again the tears flowed. The smile was gone.

Eye contact with the crowd did not assist my journey anymore. I felt alone in a crowd of fellow runners, analogous to the feelings of loneliness described by my clients who are affected by a condition like depression or anxiety: though support was around me, I felt isolated.

I wanted to stop so much. There were five miles left at this point and I knew it would be another hour of limping. I strategized. Through the tears, I just focused my mind on one mile at a time. It was similar to breaking down a goal into smaller tasks. If you focus on building the entire object, it seems daunting; taking one piece of the puzzle at a time seems more doable. I used every ounce of concentration. For each mile, I asked myself: What part of the city was I in? Had I ever walked this part of New York before? I hyper-focused on the architecture, the style of houses I ran past, anything to distract me from the pain. I used my curiosity to focus, in excruciating detail, on anything around me but my leg. If I focused on my leg, I would be swallowed by the negativity.

Eventually we entered Central Park. The end was close by. I experienced pain that far surpassed even breaking my arm.

Then it was done. I finally crossed the finish line. The two years of training spent in preparing for this day were complete. I continued walking and passed the finish line. It was a cold November day. I picked up my medal and met Maureen outside of Central Park. People were shaking my hand, appreciating the accomplishment. It was inspiring.

Within days following the marathon, life quieted down. There were no more races for the season, no more prep work. Just back to old life as usual. That was okay. I had achieved something. I worked hard and have a memory of an experience to reflect on about overcoming challenges in life.

I will always use this experience to remind myself of what needs to get done if we want to be successful. Most importantly, it was not the achievement of the marathon itself that assured my inspiration. It was the experience of how much we can change our bodies and our minds if we look deep into ourselves and recognize the potential of our human capability. We all have something good to give in this world.

Sometimes we just need a few extra tools to get there.

CHAPTER TWO

YOUR THOUGHTS—NOT ALWAYS YOUR BEST FRIEND

You are driving casually along the highway, on your way to work as usual on this sunny Monday morning. Your morning brew in one hand, steering wheel in the other. Out of nowhere, a car comes veering into your lane and you have to slam on your brakes!

Now, I will go out on a limb and say for the most part that your first reaction probably was not something pleasant about this driver. Why? Because according to you, he almost caused an accident!

My first question is: How do you know if only five minutes before you ever encountered this speeding driver, he may have received a call from the hospital nearby informing him his father has just minutes to live? This is his last chance to see his ailing father before he passes. If you knew that, would you be more forgiving?

When I walk down the street and accidentally bump into someone, or even make eye contact, why does the person treat me as if I have "beef" with him? It seems to happen especially at night. I am walking by myself minding my business when, with the slightest degree of pressure, I bump someone. That person may turn around and make a derogatory statement about me. He might even ask if I possibly did it on purpose, almost appearing as if he wants to escalate the situation! Is this not how many of the conflicts that become our sad news stories begin?

I could be at the supermarket, the movies, or the Department of Motor Vehicles. I see the line where I am supposed to be and walk towards it. I enter the line, but in an instant of awkwardness, it appears I end up in front of someone who believes I may have cut her off. Maybe I did. Am I mistaken or am I getting a look of death? A look that says if her fantasy were reality, I probably wouldn't live to tell the tale. Or, if I were alive, I'd have probably been tortured and buried in the desert somewhere.

All of the above are examples of familiar daily experiences that happen to everyone. They take up only a fraction of our thoughts each day. Each most likely includes thoughts where a person tells the story of her day to a loved one.

- "Hi honey, I'm home. Let me tell you about this jerk who almost killed me on my way to work!"
- Or: "I gotta tell you about this guy who bumped into me ON PURPOSE. I almost got in a fight!"
- Or: "Let me tell you about this GUY who cut in front of me in line at the DMV today. I was so ANGRY!"

YOUR THOUGHTS—NOT ALWAYS YOUR BEST FRIEND

In our daily lives, people either experience or share moments where their automatic thoughts lead to negative thinking, most likely as our first instinctual response. It is pretty rare when folks tell me a story that went like this: "Hey honey, this guy cut me off while driving sixty-five today. He looked like he was in a big hurry, probably trying to get to a hospital or something. Maybe one of his loved ones is sick."

Or: "Hey honey, this guy accidentally cut in front of me in line at the DMV. I was waiting an hour and he showed up, totally in the wrong line. But you know what, he looked cool and nice. He probably didn't mean to be a jerk. And you know what happened? We got into a conversation and it turned out we both love that same indie band. We learned we even went to a few of the same shows at the stadium before. What are the chances?! I took his number and email down. Next time that band comes to town, I'm going to ask and see if he wants to go to their concert."

My question is, so why don't we? Why do we automatically take the first course of thoughts rather than the second one?

From couples arguing at home about each other's perceived intentions due to poor communication, to people on Facebook jumping to conclusions about the news or latest political intrigue, we are surrounded by folks who make assumptions. And, as I said, it's infrequent that those assumptions focus on passing along good news about each other.

As a psychiatrist, I have come across an unfortunate array of mental illnesses in my patients. On a daily basis, I see patients suffering with illnesses ranging from depression to anxiety to bipolar disorder and schizophrenia. A common denominator in these disorders is that they all shape the patient's thinking to some extent. This week, someone will come into my office and tell me a story of a person or a situation where another person either did something to him, which caused intense emotional pain, or he avoided doing something, to prevent his own anticipated negative reaction, because he assumed the experience might cause intense pain.

Let us take the common example of how our thoughts and the action of thinking actually affect our lives and our well-being. When defining anxiety, a common example is a person who has an intense fear of flying. People with this fear of flying envision, or have the thought, that if they fly in a jet, it will blow up or crash and burn. As a result, they experience an emotion known as "anxiety." When anxious people choose a behavior to skirt around or minimize their symptoms of anxiety, we call that "avoidance." As a result, they do not fly. These people may consider themselves happy because they are not experiencing the anxiety that comes with just thinking about flying. But are they truly happy?

- What if they are up for a promotion at work that requires traveling?
- What if they meet a great person who wants to go on a Caribbean vacation?
- What if their bucket list dream is to see the Great Wall of China?

Last time I checked, you have to fly to get to China. So ultimately we have a choice. Some folks are going to continue to shrink their worlds to the extent they are avoidant for the sake of the anxiety. Others are going to delve into the discomfort, identify these thoughts as "maladaptive," and go DO something about it.

How about the people who come in sad because they think their boss doesn't like them, the boy at the candy store doesn't think they are cute, or they'll never get that promotion, the job, the anything. What happens here? Folks all around the globe have automatic thoughts, primarily negative, to assume why something does not happen. Where do these thoughts commonly go? Inside—with the typical understanding that the reason something did not happen is that "I am NO GOOD. I am not smart enough, good-looking enough, talented enough, or the anything enough!" And so we have negative thoughts again, causing an emotion called sadness, and behavior that may include social isolation, lack of appetite, poor sleep, low energy, and loss of interest in pleasurable activities.

And then I pose this question to my clients…
HOW DO YOU KNOW THAT??
How do you know the plane is going to blow up?
How do you know you didn't get that promotion because you think the boss doesn't like the suits you wear?
How do you know that driver who cut you off is a bleeping bleep!
You don't!

But, alas, understanding the means by which our thoughts play tricks on us and keep us negative—making us hostages to the kidnappers I call our "minds"—requires extensive groundwork. If we accept our thoughts truly as the truth all the time, we are being barraged on a daily basis by negative experiences. And these thoughts do not have to be just about planes or bosses. They can be simpler musings about why our partner did not clean the dishes or scrub the bathroom, or why the cable guy did not show up on time. The news aids in making us feel validated that a certain group or race is the "enemy." All of these interactions, to the smallest detail, at some point lead to an assumption. But, as I pointed out, assumptions may not have our best interests at heart. An accumulation of these thoughts and assumptions can change our well-being. They can make us anxious, avoidant, angry, and downright depressed. And you know what, maybe the girl who rejected my approach today did so not because I am unattractive but simply because she is engaged and doesn't wear her ring to work.

Summer 1991, 12 years old. I am 12 years old and there is a pair of pliers an inch away from my testicles. I cannot move away from them because there are two kids holding me, not allowing me to move. I have been playing basketball with three Russian kids and mocking them for not belonging in America. Up to this point in my life, Italian and Jewish people have made up the majority of my neighborhood's population, but the Russian migration into Brooklyn has begun.

With my youthful "wannabe" tough guy attitude, I thought that dominating on the basketball court involved, as we would say, "talking shit" to the kid covering me. Well, after a few pushes, his two friends grabbed me while our angry friend pulled out a pair of pliers and slowly and methodically stated that he was going to pull my "balls" off with his instrument of pain. I would say pretty surely that I was crying in intense fear. The pliers rubbed softly over my shorts. The images ran through my mind. I rotated my hips to move my manhood away from the pliers. His point was made. His goons released me and walked away.

Spring 2006, 27 years old. "Is there a Mr. Jones?" I have just called in my last patient before lunch at a clinic in West Philadelphia. "Hey Doc," Mr. Jones replies. He stands up, and although I am five-eleven, Mr. Jones towers over me with a frame of a good six-five, two hundred and forty pounds. As we enter my section of the clinic, Mr. Jones wraps his hulking arm around me as if we are ole pals going way back. As we walk, he yells out repetitively, with no disregard of the discomfort of what he is asking, "Yo doc. There ain't gonna be no bitches in this room right, can't have no bitches with me." Wanting to laugh from the maligned honesty Mr. Jones is applying, I respond respectfully that I will be the sole physician in the room. In the room, I am told a great story of Mr. Jones' prowess a few nights back, when he picked up one of Philadelphia's best call girls. In the examining room, Mr. Jones undoes his pants. Finally, for the first time in my life, the purest appreciation of practicing safe sex is less than six inches from my line of sight. Coming out of his penis are copious amounts of thick milky cottage cheese-like discharge. As I reassure Mr. Jones that we can treat this, he looks and with a hint of sarcasm says, "Hey doc, she looked clean."

Fall 1996, 18 years old. "Johnny, you're not going to kill yourself, are you?" I am sitting on the floor of my hallway of my college dorm. I feel despondent and frustrated, and one of the few sorority girls who actually seems to have a heart provides me with this surprising question. It's been a few months into college. I do my work. I stay disciplined, which includes following my routine for success. I do not drink. I do not party. I do not take drugs. But I am alone.

YOUR THOUGHTS—NOT ALWAYS YOUR BEST FRIEND

I have become fortunate that many of the attractive girls in my dorm have become "friendly" with me, but no one asks me out.

I thought being a nice guy, treating women with respect, and opening doors would lead to being so adored. I am so different from the typical "asshole" that girls complain about. So then what the heck? Why do they only want to be my friend? When I speak to girls, I talk about becoming a doctor, loving my family, and my passion for movies. All while the girls are putting makeup on in the dorm room, getting ready for a frat party. Something's not clicking! Why aren't these girls realizing that my cultural education and future-oriented goals are worthier than playing beer pong at a warehouse?

The next week, my friend Sonya finds me lying frustrated on the floor. I ask questions probably a little too existential for a girl prepping for a sorority party. So she responds with a question I've never thought I would hear. Am I thinking about killing myself? No. At this age, I just have no other means to communicate my sadness and frustration that I haven't figured this social thing out yet. My thoughts are negative, which leads to this emptiness.

When I reflect on my budding developmental issues and these stories, I realize the extent to which my automatic thoughts were causing me grave frustration. As a youngster growing up in Brooklyn, I made assumptions about others' cultures while trying to utilize aggression to avoid accepting the assimilation of groups I had never spent much time with before. There was an angry sense that this was my area, the area of my people, and others didn't belong. What if I had never been exposed to a multitude of cultures? Could I have become a person who discriminates and develops other emotional and behavioral issues as a means to adapt? By recognizing the problems inherent in making culture-based assumptions about people, I have been able to live a more flourishing life, learning about others' history and food and enjoying the special points of cross-cultural connection that bring people together.

If we always assume we can judge folks by their appearance, we are simplistically reducing people to judgments that may not be close to their true personas. How many times have you made an assumption about the tattooed person, the interracial couple holding hands, or the nerdy guys like me with thick black glasses? The world is a closed-off place if we do not let folks in and really learn the "truth" of what makes life special and unique. Assumptions with negativity only allow the vile opinions in our heads to seep into our emotions and create a invisible layer that prevents us from learning about others.

Mr. Jones impulsively allowed his sexuality to flood his healthy consciousness and made a decision to have relations with a woman without protection. Though this did not particularly affect his emotions, there was still a negative outcome because he did not use his common sense to avoid a scenario that could cause health issues. Assumptions not only affect our emotions, but can lead to other poor outcomes as well.

In college, I made poor assumptions that I had all the tools to get a girlfriend and became so somber that someone thought I might commit suicide! I was too primitive and sad to utilize my peers and my curiosity to learn about what I was doing wrong and how to enhance my possibilities. I neither showed curiosity nor sought mentorship to improve. Sometimes, when stuck within an assumption that something SHOULD happen, we lose sight of asking others for assistance to become more mindful of what's not working and develop the skills or tools to do better and improve.

What should we do to avoid falling into harmful assumptions?

Clients come see me all the time, whether it's the adults I see, the parents of the kids I see, or even the kids themselves. Every day, I will speak to clients about the way they have been hardwired to think and connect their thoughts to their feelings. When we are talking about our thoughts, we have to start with working toward humility. No one will pass this stage if we cannot begin to believe that our thoughts are not always our best friends. We must begin to accept that even our deepest-rooted thoughts may not be correct, and that they only feel so strong because our parents taught us, our school taught us, or we taught ourselves what made sense at the time.

But all of this reinforcement by our families and societies does not necessarily mean that a thought is true. One of the most fascinating experiences of those having a panic attack is the sensation of impending doom, as if we are going to die. How much more real can that get? But guess what: as far as I know, healthy people do not die of panic attacks, and that impending doom eventually goes away. Good luck telling that to someone in the moment! The only thing that a person having a panic attack wants is to get to the closest emergency room ("ED"). That person eventually goes to the ED, and is soothed because he feels safe. Eventually such persons are discharged, most of the time panic-free.

In my office, I begin with educating my clients about the importance of understanding how our minds play tricks on us. The sooner we begin to believe this, the faster we are on our way to overall optimal health. I ask you to begin today. Do not put it off. Begin examining your own thoughts during the day, asking yourself:

- "How do I know that's true?"
- "Am I making an assumption here?"

A helpful catchphrase to memorize is, "What is the evidence for my thoughts?" If you so choose, you can actually become your own Sherlock Holmes, like a detective for your own mind.

- What is my evidence this plane will blow up?
- What is my evidence my boss turned me down for the job?
- Is it really because I do not wear fancy suits every day?

Mr. Jones, who assumed he could not get an STD from a prostitute, and my 18-year-old self, who assumed that girls should be enamored of guys who talked about fancy schmancy art, both experienced consequences. His STD and my emotions, specifically my depressed mood, were the result.

As we work from chapter to chapter, a constant and recurring value is the understanding that low mood and/or anxiety impairs us, stealing time away from pursuing success, growth, and inner happiness.

Do not be hard on yourself. These skills can take weeks to integrate. Once you feel you can become mindful of your mind's tricks that cause anxiety or stress, then I want you to begin adding other skills to avoid the negative emotions caused by your thoughts. The next skill is called "choosing to think about what you want to think about." Put simply, what this means is that if I am going to avoid going on a subway to Manhattan because I have an automatic thought that the train will become stuck in the tunnel forever, I will first recognize I have no evidence that the subway is going to be stuck forever and I will then replace this thought with what I would like to think about, such as the amazing restaurant I am going to tonight with my wife.

Over time, you can become more skilled at focusing on positive aspects of your journeys, your upcoming experiences, or just the moment, especially as your mind is less cluttered by negative automatic thoughts. We, together, will begin the journey of becoming less anxious, sad, and angry, leading to a newfound space in our minds for improving ourselves.

I continue to work on the skills every day. At this point, I perform them automatically. My mind is always examining my thoughts to ensure that, at this moment, they are only beneficial for me. Otherwise, I throw them in my mind's trash bin to ensure that no unnecessary anxiety or mood change develops. I have work to take care of, friends and family to see, and ideas to continue expanding my success. There's no time to wonder if some person just cut me in line. I am using the time to think about the next idea for another book, which new park in Brooklyn I would like to visit, or what new exercise I want to try at the gym.

TAKEAWAY POINTS

- We all have automatic thoughts daily that impact our emotions.
- These thoughts affect your friendships, your work, and even your self esteem.
- Practice becoming better at recognizing if a negative automatic thought is developing into a negative emotion.
- Begin using, "What is my evidence?" to evaluate if your thoughts are true or assumptions.
- When you feel a negative emotion coming on, master the following attitude to stay positive: "I am choosing to think about what I want to think about."

CHAPTER THREE

DON'T HAVE ANYTHING GOOD TO SAY? DON'T SAY IT AT ALL

It's Friday afternoon and your co-workers are all asking what's happening after five o'clock. Someone suggests happy hour. You think this is ample opportunity to blow off steam after work—a chance to laugh and be silly. So you decide to join them. At the bar, discussions begin. A female colleague begins making disparaging comments about other women walking into the bar. She says, "Ewwww, look at that girl's outfit. She cannot pull off that dress."

A male colleague begins talking about his boss. "That arrogant bastard. He doesn't know how to run the business."

Later that weekend, you decide to visit your parents. It is nice to catch up with them and see how they are doing. Dinner begins. Your father chimes in, "How long are you gonna stay at that job? Why don't you quit and go back to school."

When finished, your mom adds, "You look so thin! Aren't you eating?!" You suck it up and take it because these are your parents, you want to be respectful, and this is what they do.

Finally you are out of their home. You go back home and ask your partner to come over. You are hoping for a chance to relax, maybe watch a movie or the latest episode of your favorite television show. Things seem okay, but a question arises: "How come you haven't done the dishes yet?" You are thinking, *This is not what I need right now.*

You reply, "It's been a long day. I'll do them in the morning." A gentle smile and a pause.

Your partner continues, "Yeah, I don't understand how you can just go to sleep in your home knowing the dishes aren't done." An argument ensues over the dishes, which leads you to search for something possibly derogatory to say to chastise the person you love most.

Then it begins.

You begin changing how you use your language. One happy hour a year later, you are complaining about your boss, the outfits of the other patrons, and the lack of overall appreciation for your efforts at the office. When you are with your parents, you ask them how they are doing and comment on how they've gained weight. You say they probably got diabetes because of all the doughnuts they eat. When your phone rings and it is your partner, instead of answering, as you did when you started dating, with a warm, "Hey honey, how are you?", you blast, "WHAT?! I'm at the mall, you're bothering me!"

DON'T HAVE ANYTHING GOOD TO SAY? DON'T SAY IT

What's happened here? Were all these folks always this negative? Is this really what healthy human banter is supposed to be? This session is about language and its effects on our happiness and potential for success. Every day, all day, folks are using words to complain, agitate, express frustration, and argue as a means of self-expression.

At a bar, how come it's not: "Hey, let me tell you about my boss. I know he was pretty pissed off at me today because I did not hand in my work on time. I know for next week, I have to start that project earlier to ensure it's done by the deadline."

Or at your parents' house: "Hey mom, how's your diet doing? If you like, I will look into a local gym for you and see if there are any discounts."

And lastly, at home with your partner: "Honey, I know I did not do the dishes, but I am tired and I will finish them tomorrow. It looks like you are mad at something, so I would rather you tell me what's going on as opposed to using the dishes not being done to let me know you are annoyed at me."

How come these are not the topics of these situations? Why are the folks at the bar not asking each other about new movies, museums, or upcoming trips? How come your parents do not ask about your passions? How come partners start fights by using the dishes as a means to begin the dialogue?

Language is such a connection to our emotions. If we are negative, sad, resentful, and angry, many times we will choose to use the above styles and specifics of language to feel connected. We find comfort in friends who listen to us complain and vice versa. Parents make irritating comments because they have nothing positive to share for themselves. Partners begin fights to maladaptively communicate that they are annoyed by something in the relationship.

How about social media?

Avenues like Twitter, Facebook, and even the comments sections of news articles are havens for negative language. People spew derogatory, simple jargon in trying to get their points across. Twitter has seen such a surge in negative language; some folks have called it the angriest place in the Internet. I myself recently posted a Facebook comment about how my progress was moving along nicely with my marathon training, and an old friend of mine took the opportunity to comment that he felt I was boasting. Negativity at its best behind the realm of a screen.

A patient states, "I guess I am just an anxious person." I reply, "Well, I guess I cannot help you. If you were a 'person with anxiety,' then maybe, but if you are an 'anxious person,' you have pretty much defined yourself, and that is much more challenging to work with."

This is just a simple example, yet to me is so poignant. How we use language to describe ourselves is a crucial factor in determining our happiness. There *is* a huge difference between the two statements. Saying you are an anxious person sounds absolute, as if you are doomed to be this person forever and ever. *But*, if you are a person with anxiety, you can become a person without anxiety with simply the right treatments and outlook, and that is much more manageable to work with. The idea of optimism and the possibility to change are there.

And just like our above examples, patients too will come in and only utilize negative language to describe themselves or their situation:

- "It's hopeless."
- "Nothing will ever change."
- "It makes me so friggin' pissed off!"

I commonly find that the folks with the most negative word usage lean towards greater daily irritability and risk for depression. Like our automatic thinking, usage of language can invariably shape who we are, whom we hang out with, and how we move forward in this world. Over time, if we face a stressor and our first instinct is to use our language to communicate how it stinks and it hurts us, then we are only further increasing our risk of negative emotions. Folks who are happy and free of anxiety and depression are optimistic with their language, comment on the strengths folks display, and utilize language to communicate healthy, motivating ideas and strategies to master stressors. When they face a stressor, they utilize their experience to master it and along such lines will use neutral language to appreciate the stressor has occurred. Furthermore, because they are not full of negative thoughts, they are freed to use their healthy thoughts to find strategies to overcome the stressors.

Part of my therapeutic process with patients is to help them acknowledge how, within their appreciation of having anxiety or depressed symptoms, they use negative language to describe these feelings. Hopefully, the plan is for them to acknowledge that they are stuck from moving forward with growing because they are unable to utilize speech for optimistic communication, such that, going forward, they will use positive language in attempting to generate a sense of excitement about their potential new selves.

Summer 2002, 23 years old. I am being beaten to a bloody pulp by my cousin's childhood friend. This gentleman does not know I am his childhood friend's cousin. He only knows I disrespected him on the basketball court and he cannot tolerate his anger. I have used vile language to communicate my manhood: "You can't hold me!" "You're too slow old man!"

At such a young age, I use basketball as a means to lift my self-esteem and I use my mouth to chastise and belittle this guy, in the hope of embarrassing him and hearing others praise my skills. He invites me to the bathroom to "talk." I am one month away from entering medical school. I have made it. I am untouchable. My confidence is at an all-time high. I have starred in commercials. My ticket out of the streets has been validated.

But my street smarts have been blinded by this false confidence.

What a mistake.

I walk into the bathroom and decide, out of guilt, that I will apologize to him. As I begin to speak, and go to hug him, he connects with a right hook. He punches and punches again. I feel nothing as my body moves into shock. I only know I need to get out of this bathroom. I kick the door to communicate something is occurring in the bathroom. At this point he is choking me from behind. My friend opens the door to see the chaos. He shoves the guy off me and he runs out of the building.

I don't blame him.

My cockiness was unacceptable and could have turned into a grave outcome. In the moment, at twenty-three years old, my face is unrecognizable to my parents from the multitude of punches landed. My nose is broken AGAIN. Both eyes swollen nearly shut. At this age, I am still not mindful enough from past experience to predict the possible outcomes of my inappropriate verbal behaviors. I am forced to learn the hard way that we may repeat the past when we use negative language as an inappropriate tool to feel good about ourselves in the moment.

Summer 2005, 26 years old. Two weeks after returning to New York from rural Pennsylvania, where I was working for four weeks, I receive a call. It is an administrator from my medical school. He informs me I failed this clinical rotation. I failed because, according to the Medical Director I worked with, I was unprofessional in the manner in which we worked together. Simply put, he did not like the way I spoke to him in front of a patient and he was absolutely right. That was a big no-no.

The administrator continues to inform me that, due to this failure, I may not graduate with my class. How I hear it is that my medical career is in jeopardy. I ask for help. I request he look at my grades in previous rotations (mostly honors) and question how this grade can be possible. He is unwilling. He finds the grade given to be valid. I can't go back and be more mindful of the way I spoke to the director. Again, my impulsive use of language gets me into a pickle. I am helpless. I wish someone has the power to overturn this decision, but it appears it is up to me, myself, and I to figure it out. The brain is a fragile organ. The next year of my life becomes tragic.

Late Summer 2005, 26 years old. I tell the neurologist I am having these strange headaches and tingling along the side of my left leg. He tells me he will run the appropriate tests, but damn, being a medical student is a bad thing when you yourself have symptoms. I plead, asking him what it may be. He tells me he has to rule out a brain tumor. I am crying outside his office, informing my parents of the possibility. At the same time, I am calling the office in rural Pennsylvania, desperately seeking out other clinicians I worked with to ask for their support to have the failing grade changed.

A few weeks go by, what feels like years. The other doctors in that office, with whom I have formed great relationships, agree there is no way I should have failed this rotation and advocate for me. Their input alters the rest of my life. "Kill'em with kindness," my father taught me one day at the young age of six, sitting in Dominic's bar in Niagara Falls. I am unaware of whether my father at this time is an alcoholic or not. Regardless, this saying will be my favorite saying of my life to this day and a staple of who I am. I will learn later, when emotional, that doing something kind for someone will ease our coping with our emotional impulses.

Back to the brain tumor. Tests come and tests go and they are all negative for what we call an organic etiology. But what's with all these strange pains and headaches?

Early Fall 2005, 27 years old. And then it happens. I am at a meeting with retired boxers in Manhattan, discussing the long-term prognosis of fighters who have retired. And slowly, the world becomes strange. I feel weightless. The room begins to spin. My chest tightens. The overwhelming sensation that I am having a heart attack comes to my mind.

I need to call someone who is close to me. For the last few months, I have been dating a young sassy female named Kristen. I call Kristen to tell her that I am heading to the Beth Israel Emergency Room. She sounds frustrated that I am asking her to leave her networking meeting with a famous person's son to come to my rescue.

I am evaluated and cleared. No heart attack. This will be the first of three visits to the emergency room throughout the next year, due to chest pain and the fear that I am having a heart attack. A month later, while working at the NYU inpatient psychiatric unit, I re-experience the feelings and again head to the ED. My head is crushing me. More neurological tests. I actually have a lumbar puncture done—which, if you are not aware, is sticking a needle into my spine to test the fluid in the spinal canal for other neurological conditions. Looking back, I can't believe I allowed a medical student to stick a needle into my lower spine!

Things worsen. I begin to not want to leave places of comfort. I fear driving alone. I fear going on subways, planes. *I am a patient.* I have a mental illness and it is called panic disorder.

One of my best friends is getting married in California. I have to lie to him that a play I am doing at this time conflicts with the day of *his* show, when in fact there is no way I am getting on a plane. Sorry Joe.

The day of my interview for residency following medical school is happening. I am cool. I am in Dr. Stern's office and I really want to train here to become a psychiatrist. As soon as I sit down, it comes. My mind is crushing

DON'T HAVE ANYTHING GOOD TO SAY? DON'T SAY IT

and sweating. I become dizzy, but I fight. I talk to my brain and tell it to shut up, that it will not overcome what I have worked for all my life. I will never know if Dr. Stern knows that I am having one of the worst panic attacks of my life, right in his office, but I am accepted.

Now, it was off to take care of this disorder. I went on medications that took the edge off, but without knowing therapy, I was also doing therapy on myself. I acknowledged where the attacks occurred and what my brain told me to avoid. And I said, "No way!" Repeatedly. I just amped myself up. Where I became uncomfortable, I stayed longer. When the thoughts came, I told them, "No matter how hard you try, I will win. There is no evidence I will die." If my body told me, "You need to get off this train," I smirked and stayed on the train till the end of the line. If my mind wanted me to pull off on the side of the road and call my parents for reassurance, I sped up. I used my inner voice to assure me that life was not over. *I will think about what I want to think about. I have this condition and I am going to persevere.* Positive speech. *I am twenty-seven years old. Again, there is no evidence I will die.*

My girlfriend at the time broke up with me. It was a burden on her and I will always go on to appreciate what we call in my field caregiver burden, the burden the family members of folks with mental illness experience. We were too young for her to have to deal with what I was going through and she was too driven. I get it.

Looking back, I know it all started after getting the phone call that I failed the rural rotation in Pennsylvania. Man, did I have some aggressive thoughts towards that doctor who failed me. But it was my fault. I was not mindful of the manner in which I spoke to respected, older physicians. Maybe it was the growing up in Brooklyn thing. Regardless, it happened. I suffered severe consequences, including developing a mental illness. I learned a thing or two in the year 2005.

Each and every day, we overhear folks using words to express emotions. Language can be defined by the tone of our speech, and then specifically by the words chosen. Just as we can have automatic thoughts to make assumptions about the world around us, usually to help us make sense of our world, so is language another mechanism that we use to cope. When the lady at the cashier is not getting the service she wants, she will raise her voice with a direct tone to get her point across. Sadly, if the woman gets what she wants, she has learned that this is an effective way to cope with stress.

When I was a child, trash talking was a means of being cocky and belittling those you felt below you. Looking back, I am happy I got my butt kicked! I learned talking to others like this could lead to catastrophic results. Who knows what people are out there in the world? As an adult, someone I said something to could have had a gun and there would be no escaping.

DON'T HAVE ANYTHING GOOD TO SAY? DON'T SAY IT

As a young adult working at the clinic in rural Pennsylvania, my supervisor did not appreciate my impulsive humor. I should have left my tone for one of my future improv or stand-up acts. I should have been mindful of my surroundings and recognized that it is not polite to speak out of turn to a supervisor like this. I reflect and appreciate how that one moment induced a two-year history of panic attacks!

I want you to put this book down and begin reflecting on how you describe yourself.

Think specifically of the words you use to folks in your life about how you are doing and where you are in life. Be truthful. Be honest. Recognize if you place a lot of negativity in these descriptions. How far off are you from:

- "Yeah, I did not get the job, but there is probably a good reason they chose the other person."
- "Yeah, she did not call me back. It's cool. She seemed great, but I guess we are just not a good fit for each other."

Sometimes, when you feel the reasons for not getting a job are unfair (for example, inter-office politics), you may even have a "good" reason to use negative language. Don't let that situation get the better of you. I agree life can be quite unjust, but getting angry, devastated, or hostile with language usually will not facilitate getting the next job or promotion. Even worse, badmouthing the company may get back to Human Resources or peers—and impact your chances of advancement when the next position becomes available.

Now move forward. Look closely at the way you use words about the external. Are many of your descriptors negative? How do you describe your job, your friends, and your fellow employees? When you speak to friends, look at the topics you choose. Do you speak vilely of your local politicians, your favorite sports team, or those pesky kids outside your apartment?

What I am getting at is that I need you to understand that you have control over your words and your words shape your emotions. When your emotions are heightened, especially by negativity, that means there is less room for healthy positive thinking, less room for creating healthy strategies, and less room for making yourself available for an avenue towards success. If you go home each night and before sleep your mind is agitated by all the things happening to you that appear negative, there will be no room for the healthy part of your brain to present new ideas and new strategies to overcome your conflict.

My patients are provided with homework when they go home, so that they slowly begin checking in on themselves about the way they spoke to anyone they encountered in the week. Did negativity become part of their language? If they did not get what they want, do they raise their voices and use an angry tone to try to get what they wanted? Did it work?

With the parents of the children I treat in my practice, I ask them to monitor the means they use to discipline the children. On certain occasions, I will be fortunate enough to see it in person. I comment, "I notice that you raised your voice when you spoke to your child. Does that work?" Most times they say NO! I then ask, "Well why do you keep trying it?" We are all prone to anger when frustrated about life, and many times we use language to present our frustrations. But this anger leads to consequences (remember my stories)—and, worse, leads to only more negativity in ourselves. As we become older and life becomes harder, we become frustrated at times when things do not go our way. Starting at a young age, if we are taught through role models or feedback to raise our voices when angered, that anger can become part of our hard drive. It will then shape our psyches. Many will become anxious and others will become depressed when conflicted.

I want you to begin practicing using your language to describe things positively. Even if you are anxious, there are more neutral means to communicate—for example, "Such and such makes me nervous but I am working on it and I want to get better." When sad, instead of "I am so depressed," we can comment on the specifics that make us sad and acknowledge them, but try to move away from integrating the emotions. We will work on emotions in a later session, but trust me when I say that a lot of our move towards a happier self begins with the power of language. Becoming mindful of our language can instill in us the tools to talk back to ourselves with a healthier self to fight back the negativity.

The only person's language you can control is yours. You can decide if you want to argue, complain, or make fun. It takes two to tango. Look where it got me at times when I was younger. Be my guest and speak that way if, in the moment, it makes you feel better. Ultimately, however, deep inside those words there is an aspect of anger. If it persists, that anger will always risk creating unhappiness and limiting life success. We want to find means to communicate in a neutral tone, through which we can leave a dispute without allowing the negative emotions to carry us for the rest of the day.

TAKEAWAY POINTS

- Language is key to our emotional state.
- Only you can control what you speak about as well as the tone (and this includes social media).
- Begin to recognize if you commonly use language negatively.
- Begin to recognize if the topics you choose to speak about are negative as well.
- Begin to integrate more neutral emotions in your speech.

CHAPTER FOUR

THAT EGO HAS GOT TO GO

Ah, the celebrity life. Doesn't it look amazing? All our famous folks are perceived as invincible. They get to go where they want, act how they want, and be who they want. They get validated every day from the crowds of people who wish they could be them, know them, or just hang out with them for even a few minutes. When a friend on Facebook poses with a quick pic of a celebrity, we like their post because, for a quick moment, that friend must have been doing something special that we were not. That friend's ego for that moment is elevated because he, for that one minute, was on the level of that celebrity.

On a more mundane level, the envy of and wish to be someone else is visible in all settings. At high school, we have the jocks and the cheerleaders. At college, it's the sororities and fraternities. In adult life, it's who has the McMansion or the new Mercedes. Every day, our stock goes up and down based on others' perceptions of us, and their desire to be someone other than themselves.

Many of us will do anything just to be near someone who we think can elevate our stock. Many of us will even take being treated awfully just to be near someone who can elevate our ego. For Pete's sake, plastic surgeons are some of the highest paid folks in the world because folks go under the knife to elevate their self-esteem to a new level.

Let's return to Facebook. Consider how we utilize social media solely to propagate our stock—while losing the ability to actually be in the moment of the experience. Folks will go to a party or a club and stand in line for an hour. When you enter the club, will you see folks dancing? Will you see folks mingling, trying to create new experiences? No! In the dark, you will see the flashes of light coming from phones of folks either updating their status locations or taking pictures to show that, for that one second, they appeared to be having fun. Once the picture is done or the status updated, folks appear lethargic and largely uninterested in participating in the activity of being at a club. Now, of course, this situation is not the case everywhere and every time, but it is an example of how social media and its importance for the ego have decimated the value of the activity being depicted. Such value resides in our ability to lose ourselves and be connected to others, to let go of the importance of the self. In essence, we are forgetting to live in the moment.

In many ways, locating value in your own status—as opposed to your relationships with others—may provide short-term gratification. It feels good to go to a club where we may get past the velvet rope, passing everyone along the way so they may wonder who we know and who they don't know. That's because showing off what we have makes us feel important—and, what's more, everyone else does it! But does it really work? When it does, how long does it last?

Especially with social media, I feel that the "status" has become the new crack epidemic. We are living to find the new quick high, just to feel for a split second that we are important.

The ego is so powerful that it can manipulate our sense of self and create a falsified world around us, just for the sake of developing a sense of self-worth. And you know what else? It sounds so exhausting! Every day, people treat folks pretty bad because they feel they can. People ignore, devalue, and are downright mean. These are folks who manifest healthy egos on the outside, but inside are fragile and fearful as eggshells, ready to crack with insecurity at the slightest opportunity. This section is about the negative aspect of our egos (ego itself is not a negative term; egos are on a spectrum). It's about talking through and learning about how much our ego and sense of self affect our everyday life. How much does our sense of entitlement negatively affect our relationships, our careers, and our emotions?

In my practice, I rarely receive calls from people who actively feel that they are on top of the world. That makes sense, right? If they were doing so well, why would they need to see a therapist? Most folks who feel validated by the world through their sense of importance rarely come to seek treatment, because their egos are elevated each and every day. Did I say this is healthy? No. For the most part, whether it's the celebrity or the master of the universe Wall Street guy, unless they are mindful of what we discussed above, they probably are not actively thinking that their behaviors may be detrimental to themselves and others—because they are getting what they want. At least for now.

The people I want to focus on here are the folks in the opposite group—the people who are developing depressive symptoms in the absence of having the admiration that they feel they deserve. One patient I remember vividly was fifty-three years old. He had had a long life of ups and downs. He felt that he was brilliant and that if there was truly anyone who should have earned a million dollars in his lifetime, it was him. Instead, over the course of his life, he had lost his wife (through affairs), his relationship with his children (through disagreements about his bad business practices), and the respect of his family because his only momentum was his ego. He would go strong and hard to the grave, abusing those close to him while looking for that monetary validation that he was special.

A younger man in his thirties came to me in quite a pickle. A Manhattan businessman, he chose to attend an

Ivy League school for college so as to have an advantage in seeking a great career. When he graduated, he felt sad that the four years did not provide the grand "high" that he had been seeking in comparison to his friends. Throughout his twenties, he pursued a career in the financial world, spending lavishly and dating as many models and high-profile women he could surround himself with, so that others could admire how amazing his life was. That didn't help his sense of emptiness. Then he bought the condo facing the park and married a beautiful woman. Again, there was no relief to his sadness. Then, in his early thirties, like his other friends in the financial world who had also slowed down, he had a child. Sadly, a year after the baby's birth, fatherhood also did not seem to make him feel exceptional.

As a psychiatrist, I can write prescriptions. I saw a young female CEO of a start-up company who was in her late twenties. She clearly had a diagnosis of attention deficit hyperactivity disorder. She was on a stimulant to maintain attention and focus so that she could operate her business. Her drive for success was quite apparent. She had not diversified in terms of ways to feel good about herself: her mood was clearly connected to the success of the business. Over time, I realized I was writing prescriptions for her on a more regular basis, not appreciating that there were months when she was receiving more dosage of her medication than she was prescribed. I identified this discrepancy. The woman was clearly abusing the medication, trying to utilize the stimulant as a safer form of cocaine to avoid having to go to sleep—so that she could work on the business to avoid feeling inadequate and to decrease her internal sense that other companies would be gaining on her if she stopped working.

In practice, a majority of these folks come depressed. They feel something is missing, a sense of emptiness. The world on a daily basis is not providing them with the affirmation that they are special, and hence they continue this endless search for something better—a different business model, year-end earnings, or a new experience that others rave about—in the hope that it will be the answer to their feelings of inadequacy. Thinking only of themselves and the importance of their own journeys, they isolate themselves from family and friends and dismiss their relationships with those "beneath" them as having no meaning.

In these cases, I try to provide support as we look inward and appreciate the patterns of each client's daily intentions and motivations. Over time in the office, in therapy, the goal is to attempt actively to have the client recognize this pattern—and the possibility that her mood symptoms are due to a cycle of living life to fulfill her ego. Typical thoughts of this type of client upon her first session in my office are:

- Automatic Assumption—Doesn't that person know who I am!?

- Negative Language—Get out of the way, you with the ugly clothes from that discount shopping mart!
- Victim Role—I am an important person and this pipsqueak is preventing me from getting ahead!

I attach these examples to show how the negative attitudes we adopt continue to be intertwined with the lives of many people who are struggling to find happiness and life success.

Now granted, you may say: what if the end goals that each of my clients is seeking are obtained? What if the older gentleman becomes a millionaire through a brilliant business plan? What if the man with the new baby becomes an investor in a new product or endeavor that he never tried before and becomes happy? What if the CEO abusing the medication is recognized as the CEO of the Year and feels validated? Yes, all of these would be wonderful for the ego, but let me ask you this: what happens to most childhood actors who are world-famous and then, as they age, are no longer as validated by the world? Most falter. Why? Throughout their entire childhood development, these child actors grow up with elevated egos—a sense that life will always be lived on this high point where people want your autograph and spend time with you. When they don't matter as celebrities anymore, we can't help but read in the supermarket tabloids about their battles with drugs or bankruptcy. They are using maladaptive means to re-live the high that they once had. Without appropriately developing a sense of a healthy ego that does not rely on outside validation, they will always remain at risk for developing depression.

Most likely, the older gentleman in our example will get his million dollars and then in some time feel as if he should be worth two million dollars. The finance man over time will most likely find the investment has become boring, not as exciting as when it was first established, and our CEO will, over a month or so, lose the excitement of the award. This is why we continue to shop and throw away even expensive items. Or why we continue to chase the "new car feel." These highs don't last long enough to continue to feel special.

The Facebook status with the picture of the celebrity, too, will be lost within a week amid thousands of new posts. That is why sometimes you will see someone upload the pic again a week later, trying to stretch out the sense of doing something important. All of these folks continue to seek another sense of validation instead of finding simpler, less grand, less exciting means to feel alive and feel a sense of self-worth. They live a very dangerous and volatile up-and-down life.

Winter 1998, 19 years old. At this age, I had little to validate myself. I was a good ball player and even that at times got me into trouble. Relationships were not my forte and anger was becoming a greater source of coping with frustration. At this time, I had declared a biochemistry major and was in the midst of taking one of the hardest subjects for those prepping to attend medical school: organic chemistry.

Now, one of my advantages in succeeding in organic chemistry was my visual-spatial skill. I love maps, and this gave me an advantage in the topic. The As came quite easy and I would subsequently go on to become a teaching assistant for this class a year later. This winter though, cocky that I was able to succeed in something that others struggled with, I attached my confidence to this nerdy achievement.

One day I was at the Greyhound bus terminal, waiting to go home for winter break. While waiting, I ran into a guy I recognized from the gym and with him were two girls. Both were fairly attractive. In the midst of starting to get to know each other, I would learn that the cuter girl was interested in a degree in science herself. Well, instead of being suave, wanting to learn more about her, and finally developing some social skills to undo my loneliness, my immaturity only came through stronger. I felt powerful around this girl—as if, being a year ahead and having already succeeded in the classes, I could "show off" my strengths to her to devalue her, just as I had been hurt (unintentionally) by other girls who had not validated me in the past.

I gloated about how easy organic chemistry was, how I barely needed to study, and how others would come to me asking how I did it. Let's just say I didn't impress her very much. Though she might have acknowledged I was bright, this style was not effective. I really believed simplistically that she would be enamored by the manliness of my grades, as if I was telling stories of going to battle and slaying the dragon. Instead, she just thought I was an asshole and demonstrated no interest in me. Instead of using a nice three-hour bus trip to talk to a cool girl, I sat alone and confused, not understanding why my strategy did not work.

Fall 2003, 25 years old. Honestly, I still think to this day that what I was doing at this time was pretty impressive (in the most humble of ways). I was in my second year of medical school and also the second lead in the Broadway show *Tony and Tina's Wedding*, all while living in Philadelphia. But again, instead of learning to work within myself and generate friendships and relationships while growing and cultivating my garden, I continued to use my successes solely as a form of self-preservation. I was still hurt from a lot of my past experiences and felt it was my due to inform people of what I was accomplishing. I still had not settled into loving myself and living in the present. I was more interested in the validation from others, and at times I would make the selfish decision.

One night, it was my friend's birthday and I was expected when done with the show to meet with my friend for his party. Well, that did not go according to plan. One of the fun aspects of our show was that it was interactive and we engaged the audience. On many occasions, some of the audience members were attractive girls and you could tell they were interested in you because you were an actor in a show. Midway through this performance, I was already setting my eyes on this pair of gals, wondering if they would want to hang out after the show. But what about my friend's birthday?

The show ended and I was correct. As I left the dressing room and came through the auditorium, they were waiting. What next? A phone call was made to my friend to convey that our director wanted us to have an after-show rehearsal, a mandatory one, due to her frustration with tonight's performance. Such a lie. A lie to take the more selfish, arrogant option for fun that night. My friend understood, but the guilt I feel even as I write this remained for some time. I made that choice because I needed the attention and the admiration, even if it was with two strangers who at that time meant nothing compared to my friendship, and even if I was at a time in life when good friends were hard to come by.

Both stories are similar. They both stem from my fragile ego and my limited sense of self-esteem, as well as my use of maladaptive, primitive means to feel temporarily good. Similar stories are told in my office. Humans are constantly looking for self-worth and validation. Especially in an age of social media, this is sadly becoming acceptable. We all want to be loved!

Both times though, I hurt someone. In the first story, I chastised someone when trying to show off how much smarter I was, and in the second, I ditched a friend's birthday because hanging out with girls was the more addictive of the two choices. In our journey toward finding our internal sense of validation, we need to become more mindful of how we handle our successes and gain insight into our motives with others. Otherwise, we may continue to lose opportunities to gain or keep relationships.

Treatment with folks who are fighting a persistent battle for validation in the world is difficult. It all comes down again to *insight*, the ability to recognize that deep inside ourselves we are using external validations to feel a sense of connectivity. Whether it's the celebrity trying to create a new barrage of publicity because his stock is waning or just the average person who treats family members, co-workers, or friends poorly to feel superior, without having that *aha!* moment that we are the ones driving this uncomfortable feeling, progress cannot move forward. We have to start looking for our true selves. The ones we are left with at night before sleep. No validations, no admiration, just our own ability inside to feel we are okay in the moment, today.

To dwell on our regrets about the past only brings up anxiety and negative emotions about the "what if." Living to accomplish something for tomorrow negates the opportunity to live for today and cherish who we have become.

THAT EGO HAS GOT TO GO

Do not live to admire others and be envious of what others have. That only creates the sense that you are trying to become someone else—what we call, on the streets, a phony. Try to avoid becoming the person who knows someone who knows someone, only in the hope that someone will admire you for being that close to someone we all admire. It will never work. This strategy will not stand up to the test of time.

I recommend that you wake up one day and admire your strengths, not focusing on your faults. Start there and begin to build. Build a life for yourself and a world that creates opportunities for you to be welcomed by others because you share an interest and a passion for something in which you excel. Create a community and a larger network not around feeling special, but around common interests and shared life experiences.

I remember one of my happiest epiphanies. I had my own *aha!* moment after thirty-two years, having become a doctor and had a really nice acting career: I realized that having a cup of coffee and reading the newspaper at a café genuinely made me happy. It was simple. I was happy I had become a person who had moved past the velvet ropes or the admiration of folks who enjoyed my show. A well-respected CEO once told me one of his favorite moments in life was having a glass of chocolate milk after a long day. I loved that. It was simple. It was constant. It was easily obtainable. Living life waiting for some "moment" that is going to bring you the inevitable sense of accomplishment you are living for is a very detrimental mode of living life.

Love life today! Be active and cultivate your garden!

TAKEAWAY POINTS

- Most humans look for some form of validation.

- Feeling empty and constantly looking for admiration by others is an emotionally exhausting way to live life. Shaming others is not an effective tool for better self-esteem.

- Practice becoming better at recognizing whether, in conversation with others or when making decisions, you are choosing the path that leads to something more prosperous for yourself versus the right choice to ensure that others remain in your life.

- Find the strength in yourself and begin to cultivate it to share, not to be admired.

- Live for today, as that is our path toward long-term success and prosperity. Let go of regrets about the past and avoid only living for tomorrow, the future we cannot predict.

CHAPTER FIVE

I AM SO MAD: DEALING WITH EMOTIONS

Day in and day out in my practice, I work with children on various skills. Frequently we work together to improve their emotional intelligence. A commonly requested skill is the skill that helps the children to recognize when they are using anger and aggression as a means to cope with their frustration. I do not want temper tantrums, I do not want throwing objects, and I do not want to see violence against their loved ones.

Now granted, this is not a perfect world, and many times I understand why my youngsters display this type of coping mechanism. Possibly their parents are not providing enough positive attention and the children recognize they will get more attention from their parents, albeit negative, by acting out. Other times, especially with adolescents, they will utilize anger to cope because the parents are not allowing them to work through gaining independence and appropriate freedom to learn to master their world. Regardless, these kids inevitably will grow up to become adults and will continue to struggle with what to do when angered. Many have only learned that anger is the best means to get what they want.

Just spend some time at a store and watch customers interact with cashiers. At some point, you will see a customer not get what he wants from the staff. He will raise his voice and make motoric gestures to display more vigor as he attempts to get his point across. He probably learned from parents—possibly through imitation—that this has worked in the past. How about relationships? How many times have you overheard or borne witness to one partner using anger to get the other to give in and become submissive to the former's wishes?

Now you may say, "Dr. Lops, in both examples people got what they wanted." This is a true statement—but to what extent will this strategy work? I am sure that at department stores and in early stages of relationships, anger may be a functional tool for dealing with frustration. However, for generating a more successful form of living—such as having more responsibility at work, becoming a manager, or having a long-term relationship that leads toward marriage—a different approach is needed. In my opinion, if anger and negative emotions are the only way you know how to cope when frustrated, many peers are not going to want to work with you or for you, and not many healthy partners will stay for long. (I say healthy because many folks with certain attributes may look for abusive, angry partners if that was what they were used to as children.)

I AM SO MAD: DEALING WITH EMOTIONS

Anger and mood dysregulation are two emotional experiences that can cause significant impairment. Both lead to outbursts, verbal aggression, and, in more severe cases, physical aggression. What commonly happens is that something from the outside world "triggers" a response in ourselves such that emotions flood our brains, undoing our mental ability to stop the unwanted behavior, and frequently such behavior will lead to consequences.

The tricky part of working with these negative emotions is that I can't simply just tell you to stop using anger to get what you want. It's been programmed. If you are a person who at the slip of the hat becomes irritable and angry, your brain without thought will activate your emotional center and you will be living as if you are in a flight or fight response. Even if the response lasts for seconds, for many the consequences can be catastrophic. So reflect if folks have told you that you have an angry side, if someone has recommended anger management, or even if, in a less severe instance, a friend or a partner has mentioned that you seem to just get angry a lot. This may be a sign your emotions are negatively impacting your daily life.

Anger is a frequent symptom of folks presenting to my office. When we make automatic thoughts about our lives, we can become angry. When we have friends who are negative and make hostile comments, we can become angry. When folks do not validate our importance, we can become angry. When we become angry, the words we use are hostile and aggressive.

When doing my assessments with my patients, keeping in mind the tenets from the previous chapters, I look for anger as a common attribute of one's way of coping with life's stressors.

A thirty-five-year-old man, a local plumber, came to my office. He was brooding in my office, telling me frustrating tales of not receiving appropriate payment from his clients. I could understand his frustration. With each tale he kept using the statement, "It just gets me so pissed off." He was a large man and actually a nice guy who was not one to resort to aggression. But because he could not work through his emotions, and everything about his job made him angry, he was becoming severely anxious. Many patients who struggle with anger inside will present with anxiety on the outside. His anger because he never learned developmentally how to self-soothe affected his general sense of calm. He ruminated for most of the day and this impacted his relationships with his family and partner. This invariably led to self-soothing though alcohol use.

Humans are not simple creatures. Folks will find ways to cope and undo their negative emotions. However, as we can see, these ways of coping, even if effective, can lead to external consequences for themselves (through substance use) and for others (as they try to direct their aggression towards others to feel better about themselves through bullying behavior).

If you remember when I got beat up in the bathroom for talking "smack" to the older friend of my cousins when I was twenty-three, his inability to tolerate my shenanigans led to his aggression towards me. Although I was beaten up pretty badly, he still was arrested and had to face those consequences. He was the opposite of my patient above. His anxiety was building up as I was showing him up on the basketball court, so that the only means he knew to deal with his anxiety (on the inside) was to display anger and aggression on the outside.

A twenty-eight-year-old female, a computer programmer who had previously been on medication for severe anger and mood dysregulation, came to my office to discuss tools to cope with her rapid expressions of anger. She told stories of folks on bicycles cutting her off while walking and triggering her anger to where she literally chased them down the street until they stopped. She screamed and berated the cyclists until they drove off. Interestingly enough, my patient as she became older recognized that she had an anger problem and was trying to minimize the consequences as a result. She was moving up at her job and had met a partner she cared for.

As I mentioned before, regulating one's mood is not a choice for most folks. She informed me her mother was verbally abusive as a child. Her anger had been programmed through, and modeled by, her mother. She appreciated learning to handle her emotions was a skill that needed practice. While she had insight, she still could not undo the program that had been etched into her brain's emotional center.

In my sessions as a clinician, it is extremely valuable if my patients can recognize that these behaviors are unhealthy to them, notwithstanding that they may get a release or "high." If someone is rigid or inflexible and unwilling to identify that these behaviors lead to consequences, then the work is that much harder. After they recognize that the behaviors are not healthy, the next step is to make the connection to the process of working with their emotions. Trying to break down and identify all the triggers can assist in beginning to replace anger as the main source of relief in stressful situations. Once that is completed, we begin to attempt over time, and with dedication, to implement healthier, adaptive tools to utilize when triggered.

Patients say this seems so hard to do, but so is doing fifty pushups in a row. Everyone is capable of doing fifty pushups, but the work and the time have to be put in to see results. Similarly, most life skills needed to be successful come from time, humility, and a lot of work. Trying to do fifty pushups is humbling right now. Learning to recognize you can become easily angered when triggered takes time, but the strength to persevere and use other tools will in time come more naturally, just as doing daily pushups will eventually get you to fifty in a row!

I AM SO MAD: DEALING WITH EMOTIONS

Many of my previously mentioned stories have included aspects where emotions, on top of other skills, were not utilized properly.

Fall 2001, 23 years old. Working in corporate America is hard! There are so many rules and politics that the constantly-present hierarchy almost resembles a caste system. I have never experienced this milieu before. I need the job to supplement my acting career and I am not sure about attending medical school at this time. I work as an administrative assistant and wow, the phone calls, the direct orders, and the inability to just go to the bathroom when I want are really stressful! Furthermore, I have to take the subway an hour each morning in the freezing cold (or, during the summer, in the 100-degree heat). I am young and have not developed the tools to handle the rigors of the daily grind in a sophisticated way.

My boss at this time was tough: direct, on the go, and not so empathetic. At some point, I recognized I was beginning to carry my emotions to work, almost like having a second layer of skin that held my negativity. I felt I was becoming shorter with folks and finding myself more agitated. I didn't have a good sense of self. My acting career, as many careers are, was inconsistent and at times stagnant. I knew medical school was a possibility, but for today, even with a bachelor's of science degree in biochemistry from a prestigious university, I was an administrative assistant and had to handle the duties of an administrative assistant. My ego was frustrated.

One morning, my boss walked over to me to address yet another deficiency in one of my duties. Like a bolt of lightning and without thinking, I said, "Just go away, Evelyn." My boss in shock indeed walked away and wow, for the moment at least, I got what I wanted! Of course, she had the last laugh: a phone call from Human Resources came and a meeting was set up. I was reprimanded and told that if this were to occur again, further actions would be taken.

It makes sense though! I was a fighter growing up. We lived on impulsive decisions, using anger and strength to cope with frustration. I fortunately had choices. I needed to apply to medical school. It provided me with the opportunity to return to school and use that time to enhance other skills I would need to be prepared for the rigors of adult life.

I was too young and primitive for the corporate world at twenty-three, and it showed. Sometimes a change of scenery is important to allow us to work on ourselves. If we cannot change our environment so easily, the only recommendation is to practice. Let's begin working on those fifty pushups!

Summer 2003, 24 years old. A road trip through America: a to-do on the bucket lists of many folks. This summer, I planned an extensive trip, nine weeks on the road to see

I AM SO MAD: DEALING WITH EMOTIONS

as many of the beautiful natural and man-made sights our country has to offer. My dad came for a lot of it going west, but the plan was to return home with two of my best friends. We went to Utah for whitewater rafting. We went to South Dakota for Mount Rushmore. We went to Minneapolis to see the Mall of America. We did a lot, but at the end of the day I was with my boys and sometimes boys from Brooklyn want to be boys. I could feel them getting antsy. We were doing too many cultural events.

As we were passing through Denver, they wanted to know when we were just going to go to a city and visit the local gentleman's club.

They knew these clubs weren't my favorite places to visit. But as the guys had been amazing in agreeing to the sights I had planned, how could I say no to their request? We found a club that appeared appealing to my friends and we entered.

I remember walking in and to the right. We were in a part of the club where there were little platforms, maybe only two feet high. The girls would dance on the platforms while the guys sat on cushions just beneath and received a more personal experience. I told my friends to sit while I was going to stand against the wall. The method to my madness was that if I stood against the wall, I would not be bothered and it would give the appearance that I was here for my friends who were sitting on the little cushions.

Yeah, that didn't work. While standing, it may have given the appearance I was trying to get the "experience" without being on the cushions, presumably to avoid giving the expected "tip." How do I know this? Well, as I stood, a tall, lanky brunette walked by. Now I am five-eleven and she towered over me, possibly from the heels she was wearing. She got close and yes, with respect, she asked for me to take a seat and promised that I would enjoy the show better. Trying to be humble and honest, I retorted that I thanked her for the gesture, but I was here for my friends and this was not my cup of tea. I was just going to stand back here until my friends wanted to leave. She scoffed and walked away.

Time went by, maybe twenty minutes, and she came back. Except this time, she got quite close to my face. Out of her mouth came: "Listen motherfucker. You better fucking sit down and start throwing some dollars down."

I was improving my emotional intelligence and means to handle this type of frustration, but I was not there yet. I leaned in towards her and said, "Listen, you Amazon bitch, I would rather be in Soho having conversation over a latte than pay to watch you dance."

She got right in my face and pushed me. I pushed back. Within seconds the bouncer came and grabbed me. Before any further aggression arose, we were thrown out of the club, fortunately without any police involvement. We went onward. This story was enough to foreclose seeking any other gentleman's establishment for the duration of our trip.

I AM SO MAD: DEALING WITH EMOTIONS

I grew up seeing a lot of violence. Though I was quite educated, it still remains a process to undo the reactions that seem to be the norm learned from my peers during childhood. I saw my father throw a man down a flight of stairs under the influence because the man did not agree with his political beliefs. By the age of fifteen, I had been shot at and robbed at knifepoint. Someone even tried to blow me up for wanting to call the cops on the local street gang, who were involved in drugs and trying to pull my friends into their illegal endeavors.

But none of this is an excuse. I cannot tell an HR manager in corporate America or the police in Denver that I became aggressive because of my upbringing. No, it requires recognizing that these are unhealthy ways to deal with the moments that trigger anger.

Working with emotions is very similar to the concept, from the first chapter, of catching our thoughts. As I have stated time and time again, understanding from an educational point of view that you have difficulty with anger that leads to behavioral consequences is always the first step towards improving the skill. If you are a kid teaching yourself how to play basketball and solely use your own feedback to improve, you are not going to develop these skills as well as you would if, say, Michael Jordan identified where you needed to improve. Worse still, if you deny feedback from others that could benefit your game, you are not going to improve your basketball skills. Half the battle consists in having the ability to welcome the feedback that your anger is too intense and leading to consequences.

The next step, after understanding the process, is to try to displace this anger away from the directed person or source of your anger and put it somewhere less toxic. Unlike working with the other tools in this book, working with emotions and anger is slightly more complicated because these skills require some assistance from friends and family. I can't change your workplace and the folks there, but with the others, we can be more involving. We have to understand if your environment is invalidating—or, in other words, if it is a trigger to your emotions.

Friends or family, in trying to help, may label your emotions as disturbing or extreme, so that you begin to think that your feelings are wrong. Well, feelings can't be wrong, they are your feelings. What we *can* work on is how we handle the feelings behaviorally. I bring this up because if those closest to us cannot support and validate why we are feeling the way we do, we will continue to have extreme reactions when triggered. As I mentioned before, we learned these emotional responses. People do not choose to grow up having anger as a means to cope with frustration.

If you find the necessary friends and family on board, let's begin catching these emotions. Begin observing when you get angry. Try not to stop the experience. Let the emotions happen and begin to describe them to yourself.

I AM SO MAD: DEALING WITH EMOTIONS

Acknowledge the emotions. Are you angry, sad, or mad? Do you recognize the physiological response? Is your heart racing? Is your chest getting tight with more shallow breaths? In the beginning, this is all I would ask. You still may have the behavioral consequence and feel guilty for your response. But the idea is first to become mindful and in tune with how your body is changing when triggered.

Once you have mentally connected the triggers with your emotions, focus on that one millisecond of time before you react. The plan will be to instill other tools that you will choose. Think of boxers and how fast those punches are coming at them. They have milliseconds to decide how to move away from the punches. If you speak to a boxer, time is much slower in the ring and they have practiced all the angles from which punches come. Even where a jab or a hook seems to arouse an instantaneous and automatic response, a choice is still being made by the boxer in a single millisecond of time. That is the same idea here. If you practice, you can take the millisecond and make a different choice. Make the choice not to tell your boss to walk away, as I did at my corporate job, or antagonize the dancer at the bar with your body language.

The tools listed below are about using what we already have: our sense. Using our sense in the moment can help us to develop the reflexes to focus on self-soothing so as to avoid using aggression.

If you are angry, you can use:

- *Your eyes.* Look at something in your immediate world, like people or a beautiful sky. Pull up an online article or pictures on your phone. Play games or chat on the computer. Watch a favorite show or movie on TV that can soothe you and distract you from the unwanted emotion.
- *Your ears.* Listen to your favorite music, play an instrument (I play the drums), or call a family member or friend.
- *Your smell.* Light a candle to soothe yourself, or make a favorite cup of tea with a nice fragrance.
- *Your taste.* Go for something that you enjoy. I always get a slice of pizza if I want to undo some negative emotions and I am hungry.
- *Your touch.* Pet your animal (we have a kitty). Take a shower or bath (cold or warm, whichever you find more soothing). Hold a squeeze-ball or any ball that is available.

These sensory distractions are what I recommend many folks utilize, but of course you may come up with others. You may also use larger, more exerting tasks to cope. You can go to the gym and exercise, play sports, or make art. The goal is the same: to gain a "pocketed skill" that you know from your practicing works for you, just as a boxer has trained himself to move away quickly from an uppercut coming forward. If you become dedicated to this skill, just as an athlete or artist is dedicated to her craft, over time you should recognize the ability to manage your emotions through healthier and less toxic options.

> ## TAKEAWAY POINTS
>
> - Anger is a normal emotion. Your "normal anger" may have been created through childhood experiences and/or from modeling a parent figure.
>
> - From time to time, anger may help you get through stressful situations AND get you what you want, but it will eventually deter you from promotions and relationships as you grow.
>
> - How we deal with anger is what differentiates us from constantly having bad outcomes versus finding means to work with emotions in a healthy manner.
>
> - Use your mind to begin recognizing when your body is responding to anger.
>
> - Practice using sensory tools to distract yourself from the anger to avoid a negative consequence.
>
> - Defusing the experience of anger and its consequences towards others and yourself is an incredible advantage when working towards happiness and success.

CHAPTER SIX

ARE YOU UP OR DOWN AFTER A NIGHT WITH YOUR FRIENDS?

Most adults do two things: we work and we pay taxes. By contrast, we have the liberty to spend our free time as we choose. The choices we make during that free time make us unique.

Deciding what to do with the valuable Friday to Monday time we have before the work week rolls around again can be overwhelming. In other chapters, we have explored how our brains operate to affect our well-being on a daily basis. This chapter is different. Here, I want to expand outside our personal borders and examine how the people we spend our valuable time with can affect our well-being for better or worse.

The science of friendships is complicated:

- Why do we choose who becomes our friends?
- What needs do particular friendships fulfill?
- How do we make friends in the first place?
- How do we keep and maintain friends?

To some extent, we all have one, two, or even a few more folks we like to call "our friends." Friends are there for us. They listen when we need them to listen to us. They are our companions in life when it comes to spending valuable time outside of our work and family—exploring the world, checking out new restaurants and new travel destinations, or trying a new hobby.

But let's look more closely at how friendships impact us.

It's Friday night and you've had a stressful week at work. The Monday prior, you reached out to a friend whom you see sporadically because you both work at busy jobs. Work has been more taxing than usual. The boss has been breathing down your neck and sheesh, you cannot wait to have this week over and just enjoy a little time to relax. You make plans by text to get together with your friend. You decide on meeting for dinner and maybe a drink afterwards. Perhaps you might catch a show together at your local music venue. On Thursday and Friday you barely make it though the workday, but you know it will all be better by Friday night.

Then it happens. On Friday around 1:00pm, a text comes through on your smartphone. It's your friend, and he communicates so emotionally how sorry he is. He has to cancel your Friday evening kickback. Maybe he's sick. Maybe he forgot Dad's birthday is the same night. Maybe a bunch of things happen. There you are on Friday afternoon with four more hours of work to finish up. All the fun plans for tonight to relax and not think about the hassles of work have been lost, flushed down the drain in a single text. You feel rejected and sad.

Examples like the above can happen in a variety of ways. Humans are people. They can be selfish and make mistakes; others don't always have our best interests at heart. Friends can lie behind our backs. They may not support us when we want to try out new experiences. They can chastise us for wanting to improve and become better people. They can even lie to us about their plans because something better came up for them. If you follow what's happening in the news, friends can even ruin business relationships, steal from us, and—at their worst—ruin marriages.

Consider your friends and connections in the social media world. Many social networking sites like Facebook have altered the original meaning of the word "friend." Who are half of these people? Do they affect us and our lives in positive ways? Do they inspire us? Do they encourage us and make us better people? Whether we assume we have more friends online or offline, there is always pressure to "consume" friends in the modern world.

What does this mean? What transpires is that we begin shifting our focus away from having a few healthy, positive friends who are truly there for us, and toward accumulating acquaintances with the intention of helping us network. Especially where I live in New York, it seems like everywhere I go, many people's "friends" are actually human opportunities to improve oneself. Not for the purpose of actual friendship, but with the idea of hoping that enough people on our "friends list" can help us get something back to enhance ME. What ends up happening is this: because there isn't as much of a true, close, human connection, it becomes easier for folks to ditch us at the last minute, cancel plans for something better, and increase our chances of feeling disappointed, rejected, and alone.

Let's change things up a bit and look a little further. Maybe you have already mastered the tools in the other chapters. You can be described as a successful person, and you have others connecting with you, wanting to be your "friend." In the past, your friends have always answered texts quickly and are practically on call, ready at any time for the opportunity to hang out at the bars and clubs where you're a well-known regular.

But what if, tonight, the plan that you the "successful friend" have in mind is less exciting? What if the plan is staying home and watching a classic, old film from the 1940s because you want to show your friends your new interest in Film Noir? Would they come over and join you? Would your "friends" be interested in spending time with you outside of what you have access to, outside of the aspects of you that could be a direct benefit to them or make their lives more exciting?

ARE YOU UP OR DOWN AFTER A NIGHT WITH FRIENDS?

Friendships play a significant role in my practice and in the field of psychiatry generally. When we complete evaluations of our patients, I perform what is called a "Bio-Psycho-Social" assessment. The "Bio" is the biological component of their presentation, i.e. their genetics and their family history, including whether any of their family members have a mental condition, say anxiety or depression. The "Psycho" portion is about the psychology of my clients, as best understood through their mental functioning and how they understand their world around them. Lastly, the "Social" aspect of the evaluation is intended to build an understanding of my clients' social world, including their family, their employment history, and their friendships.

A professional athlete came to my office and explained to me that he struggled to understand who his real friends were. He felt anxious about it because even though he definitely had "friends," he always felt somewhat uneasy about many of his friendships. If he truly needed someone to be there for him, he was unsure of the genuineness of the contacts stored in his phone. He was troubled by the idea that as he neared retirement from his sport, all the folks he had partied with throughout the years would no longer stay as connected to him as when he was younger and free to spend more money on the weekends. He felt uncertain about who would be there for him after the glitz and glamour wore off, when his life would change.

Another pro sport athlete, now retired, came to my office with a similar, complementary concern. He acknowledged that as he had played his sport, he had enjoyed having multiple folks around him whenever he wanted, assuring his ego that he was special and on top of his game. He had enjoyed telling tales of having friends he could turn to at any moment. Now that he was retired, he struggled with sadness when suddenly others were not as invested in showering him with the feedback and accolades he seemed to need to validate his ego. His friends stuck around, but he felt less important and less admired by them. He never developed other means to feel emotionally intact.

Outside of the world of athletics, a young twenty-year-old woman from my hometown of Brooklyn came to see me. Her mood was sad and she seemed to have an underlying sense of anxiety. She expressed multiple automatic negative thoughts about herself. She discovered as she became more negative that she was spending more time with peers who were quite negative themselves. She soaked up time with peers who gossiped, chastised other friends, and had a negative opinion of anyone trying to leave Brooklyn to do more with their lives. The negativity took a heavy toll on this young lady. She became so anxious that she was stuck: paralyzed by doubt from taking action in her own life, and unable to move forward with her college education. Eventually she took a leave of absence.

Once we understood her negative thinking, we were able to recognize that she solidified and reinforced her negativity through her unhealthy choice of peers. Her habit of "making fun" of everyone else became an unhealthy way to cope with her emotions. Once that was fully understood in our sessions together, I recommended she reconnect with peers with whom she shared similar interests, including certain hobbies, sports, and art activities that could nurture her growth and aid her in moving forward, as opposed to stagnating in negativity with peers who only caused further regression.

As a clinician, it is very important for me to understand my patient's inner world. Folks can develop worsening depression because they perceive or view themselves as lacking in friendship. The feeling of being disappointed consistently, or of not having friends to validate ourselves, may be a sign that our chosen friends may not be the best option for our growth. Making some changes in our social life, particularly in terms of how and why we choose our friends, can affect our overall mental well-being.

Summer 1993, 14 years old. Oh boy. Jesus is totally not going to be happy with me. If you want to know what it's like to break someone's nose, I mean truly shatter it, please follow these instructions. 1) Take about two feet of aluminum foil, 2) place the sheet with your hand squarely in the middle of it, and 3) crumble it.

REINVENT YOURSELF: ESSENTIAL TOOLS

Twenty-one years later, I can feel every piece of that nose, the cartilage shattering as I laid my first punch on someone. Dad always told me that if someone messes with you, just lay the first punch, right on the nose, and the fight is over right there. A young man on the basketball court was bossing me around, poking fun at me in front of my friends. My friends saw me, someone who ordinarily never engaged in aggression, losing my cool somewhat more that day. They took advantage: instead of using their influence on me to avoid the outcome, they only encouraged it. What friends would want the outcome of an altercation to lead to violence?! Ouch, my hand hurt for a few days!

Fortunately for my future and my career, my father's teaching point would be one I would use less often than my friends did. I think this ensured that I stayed on the straight path to success. One assault today can cost us our jobs, our relationships, and some of the things that are most important to us. My friends sought entertainment on this day, not my well-being.

Summer 2002, 23 years old. I truly think we are going to die. We're in Bob's van, a van he needs to use a screwdriver to open, and we have just gotten onto the Manhattan Bridge. It's about 3am. Mike and Jeff sit in the back, me shotgun. We veer and I ask Bob what that was about. He tells me he just cut this guy off and we almost hit him. *Damn,* I am thinking, *I am about two months away from starting a new phase in my life, entering medical school. I am purposely trying to avoid all conflict.*

But the strangest thing begins. Bob rolls down his window and I look over. This white man in his fifties who looks like a Vietnam vet type is shouting and cursing at us while driving on the bridge. I am thinking that this guy is crazy, but Bob is cursing him back. "Dude, just let it go," I say. And then it's taken to the next level. The guy swerves into us and *oh, my god, am I scared.* Bob swerves into him and here we are, this is really happening, we are bumping each other on the Manhattan Bridge and when the other driver bumps into us I can see the water below us on my side. I begin to cry. I am begging Bob to just stop and let this guy go. He obviously is not mentally stable.

We hit the apex of the bridge and begin our descent. The other driver speeds up before taking the situation to yet another whole new level. He makes a right and pulls into our lane, exactly perpendicular to us. I freeze. The man is staring at us and I am sure this guy has to have a gun. Who would be this crazy while there are four of us in the car? Bob is also at this time in his own world: I can hear him muttering under his breath. "Get out of the car, just get out of the car," he is saying to the man. I scream, "Are you nuts? If you get out of this car, you will die." He tells me he has a bat in the back.

I turn to Jeff and Mike and what are they doing? Sitting comfortably in the back playing pocket blackjack. I yell out, "Aren't you scared?" Jeff looks up and says, "Don't get so dramatic."

I look back at the guy. It feels like ten minutes, although in hindsight it's probably no more than one. We continue to stare. Then the mad driver simply goes into reverse and pulls away. All I can think is, "I gotta get out of NY. These friends are going to get me killed."

Fall 1990, 12 years old. My friends were breaking up with me. Man, I cried in front of a bunch of fourteen-year-olds so bad. It hurt.

My best friend Craig called his new high school friends over and asked to come to my house. They had all just started high school and were fourteen. I was still in seventh grade, barely twelve. The discrepancy in maturity showed and I don't blame them today, but it was rough. They wanted to start picking up girls and hanging out; I was still freaking out over the newest Sega Genesis game.

So can you picture about four guys whom you admired and looked up to, and they came into your room and literally told you they could no longer be your friend? It was like an intervention, except that when it was over, I sat alone crying in my bed. I think I never got over it. Even today, although most people consider me a social guy, I have difficulty getting too close. I always fear the abandonment.

I was lucky to have my dog Fluffy by my side. He was my friend to the end. I remember just holding him and appreciating the bond between humans and dogs. He was always there for me and never let go till the day he died in my arms. I think it's the reason I learned to value my girlfriends. I think the pain of friendship made me yearn for a solid companion.

Whom we choose to spend our time with has a significant impact on our growth. Growing up in southern Brooklyn, I was surrounded by a lot of negativity, a lot of peers dealing with family strife, and a lot of kids who used aggression and the streets to feel good about themselves. Although I had good family values, we have seen from this section and other sections that my street aggression and sarcasm led to many poor outcomes.

I still love my Brooklyn friends to death, but to develop fully as a person striving for success, I needed to surround myself with like-minded, future-oriented folks who were optimistic, positive, and supportive.

This chapter evokes many emotions for me. I have a place in my heart for those who struggle socially and have an underlying self-esteem issue arising from the fear of not having friends. As I became older, however, I learned more about friendships and what to expect. Also, in treating clients, I have seen patterns that can consistently predict how one will move forward with friends.

Who are your friends?

Take a moment and ask yourself if your friends have your best interests at heart. Would your friends put you in situations where you can grow and mature, or are you a chess piece for their playing field? My recommendation would be that if there are friends who consistently do not respect your autonomy and your growth, and selfishly place you in scenarios where even danger is a possibility, it may be the right time to bring these friendships to a conclusion. We want folks around us who can nurture us and help bring out the best in us.

What are my typical friend conversation themes?

As in the language chapter, listen to the folks with whom you spend the most time. Do they have their own personal goals for growth and expansion? If you find that, nearing the end of most conversations with some friends, you are beginning to find yourself speaking more negatively, you need to think about what the advantage of this friendship is. I am not saying that every conversation requires a discussion of how you plan to become the president of the United States, but I am looking for some sense of encouragement and positive interest in your long-term goals, travels, and dreams.

Why do I choose these friends?

We at times choose friends from whom we ourselves can gain something. Possibly we look for someone who

ARE YOU UP OR DOWN AFTER A NIGHT WITH FRIENDS?

has an exciting job or a position of power that, for example, could get us tickets to the Knicks game. Alternatively, we may choose friends who we know admire us, and we may use them as a false validation in order to feel valued by the world.

With friends in positions of power, we need to be aware that many of us use that sense of feeling important as a tool to feel important ourselves. But by doing so, it is my recommendation that you continue to work on means to feel good about yourself that are not connected to your friend—because if your friend were to leave that job or lose access to the "cool" advantages, we want to avoid becoming sad and developing a sense of emptiness. Lastly, by only surrounding yourself with friends who place a lot of value on what you can provide for them, you place yourself at risk for feeling alone if—and hopefully this does not come to pass—you can no longer provide those services.

Friendships are grown over time. If you recollect the criteria I use to define "friends," that may only amount to a few people. Well, that would be amazing! We hope to surround ourselves with a few folks who, regardless of status, power, and access to things they admire, care for our well-being; they care about our inner selves, what we stand for, our interests, and our personal growth. And they truly have our back. Our understanding of who our true friends are can allow us to persevere through our journey and find the further happiness we seek.

TAKEAWAY POINTS

- Assess if you feel better or worse after seeing your friends.

- Do your friend's conversations always tend to lean negative?

- Friends should be part of your life regardless of status and wealth.

- Good friends inspire us, not berate us for trying to expand ourselves.

- The accumulation of friendships on social media sites for status is not the path towards healthy emotional well-being.

CHAPTER SEVEN

NO MORE VICTIM MENTALITY: YOU CAN DO IT

My dad used to laugh as I was growing up when he talked about reading the newspaper. He wondered, "How come there's never any good news? They only print the bad things that happen around us."

He was right. Today, as then, we still read about what terrible stuff happened to whom, when, and where. We face a constant barrage of these incidents from the various television networks. Everyone in the news has had something bad happen to him. Don't get me wrong: if something truly bad happens to someone, we should empathize with, and feel upset by, his experience. Yet there is also a general trend toward painting all people as nothing *more* than victims—as people whose external circumstances can never be surpassed by their human potential.

This chapter is about the people who, after difficult experiences, shape their lives into their personal victim roles and invariably become "stuck." What concerns me about how folks watch the news today is that some actually find it beneficial to become a "victim." People pay attention to you. People ask, "How are you doing?" and provide a daily means to soothe you from your troubles.

How do you draw a fine line between trying to support a person who has experienced a trauma, and encouraging him or her to persevere and become stronger?

This chapter is about asking you an important question: when you look back upon the significant experiences in your life that shaped you negatively, how much were you able to persevere and move forward, versus allowing a negative experience to influence you and create a role, or a mindset, that you knowingly or unknowingly use as a crutch to avoid moving beyond your comfort zone?

Listen to conversations you share with others. Listen intently, specifically when they discuss tough times in their lives. Do they fully blame others? Do they specifically mention an event or another person as the reason that prevented them from improving or succeeding in certain aspects of their lives? Do you have conversations that sound like the blame game, too?

Listen to people of all ages talk about why they fell victim to another person or circumstance in different ways:

- When a child's teacher calls a mother to discuss a behavioral matter with her child, later he will explain to his mom it was little Joey who sits at the desk next to him who caused him to get in trouble. So, why

wasn't he paying attention to the teacher and the lesson?
- Teenagers will tell their parents they broke curfew because a friend was driving and refused to bring them home. So, why did they even get into the car that late at night?
- College students will tell their parents they failed certain courses because the teacher refused to review past lectures. So why didn't the students go to the professor during office hours to ask more specific questions?
- Young men and women in the workforce will tell their bosses they arrived to work late because the subway was running late. So why did they go out drinking on a Tuesday night?
- Middle-aged spouses will tell their significant others they cheated because their hands were tied: the cheated-on parties were not as sexually available as they wanted. So, why didn't the cheating spouses communicate their frustrations with their relationships to their partners earlier?

Invariably, the list can go on. When "bad" things happen, some people develop an inability to take responsibility; no one wants to look into himself or herself to truly understand and learn from why something happened. In my field as a psychiatrist, this behavior is called a "victim role." Many people cling to the belief that they are just passive stand-by characters in the script of life.

What is it about us humans that causes us to struggle to take responsibility for our actions or inactions? It hurts our egos too much to admit we did something wrong. You know what? I don't blame us. Because just as the person who feels victimized understands how this role can occasionally aid her, so do we also know that acknowledging our mistakes can lead to a never-ending acceptance of a scapegoat role that others can and do use to devalue us when it seems fit. If I take responsibility for showing up late to work because I had one too many drinks last night, my boss may respect my honesty. However, this admission can lead to a power shift, such that my boss can make "automatic assumptions" about me whenever I'm two minutes late in the future.

It's easy to use a negative experience from the past to validate why you have not moved forward. When this happens, the future can become a bland, limited time as you stagnate and wonder why you aren't moving forward. Stay stuck and you're likely to relive the role of the past instead of using the experience to persevere and become stronger. On the other hand, you can appreciate using your negative experience as motivation. It can serve almost like rocket fuel, making you unstoppable, propelling you toward the attainment of your goals.

NO MORE VICTIM MENTALITY: YOU CAN DO IT

The rubber hits the road when you listen to older folks, those in retirement. Not everyone reaches and obtains all their life goals. Many will share stories of the genuine moments of adversity where, for example, they persevered against the odds and opened a small business that eventually made them successful. By contrast, other elderly people will focus more on the specifics that impaired their potential. Maybe it was the government; maybe it was that car accident when they were twenty-two years old. Again, I do not devalue the reality of someone who has experienced a traumatic life event. My focus is specifically on how some will move forward despite the trauma and others will regress into a lifetime of focusing on the incident and blaming it as the reason for why their goals were never changed or upgraded.

In session, folks come with a multitude of reasons to help them justify where they are in life. Many will recognize their own shortcomings, and possibly the poor choices they made in the past that they would change if they could. Hindsight is 20/20, but at least they recognize that they themselves played active roles in reaching their current states. They also recognize how I, as a therapist, can assist them in working through certain issues so that they can try not to repeat the past again.

These folks are usually easier to work with. It is more challenging when clients come and repeat a similar story, using their sessions solely to speak of their pain regarding someone else's actions or failings.

A young lady came to session with severe anxiety. Her situation was that her neighbors owned lavish cars and threw extravagant house parties; she was angry, anxious, and having daily panic attacks because her husband only made a certain amount of money per year. With their bills for daily living expenses, they could not afford the pricey in-ground pool that she was telling her neighbors she was preparing to install. Week after week, she came to session asking for medication adjustments to work through the chronic anxiety she experienced because she was a victim of her choice of husband. His "minimal" income was not enough to validate her ego by enabling her to have an object of wealth, the pool, to show off.

We speak about ego in another section, but what was more palpable in my sessions with this woman was just how much of a victim she was—and there was no escape! If we cannot work on insight to recognize our roles in our situations, it becomes extremely difficult to work through and find the openings to our sources of happiness and contentment in the present. My patient needed her pool, and to her, that was her happiness. But what journey was she on? Her limitations to appreciating her happiness presented a never-ending battle. We all know that once she got the pool, she would just turn her attention to the next false material object that she hoped would bring her some sense of momentary happiness. In this situation and in many others, the goal is to have folks recognize that the roles they choose may give them an excuse to avoid taking responsibility.

How come my patient herself did not work to assist in getting the pool? Well, why should she? All the other "socialite" neighborhood women did not work. On the other hand, if she worked, she would obtain the pool faster. But it was easier to come to the therapist, and speak her mind about how awful her situation was, than attempt to avoid the role of the victim and make her situation better for her and her husband.

To accept honestly our roles, and the limitations to our standing in life, is the "truth" towards emotional well-being.

We all know that the situations we are born into can affect our life directions. Sadly, I clearly remember that, when struggling to find consistent acting work at age twenty-two, I berated my parents immaturely for not having more "in-the-know friends" who could make phone calls to assist my career. My parents were an easy target to validate why my career was not moving forward more quickly. I was being a victim.

In sessions with my patients, half of the battle is achieving the humility needed to appreciate the past and come to terms with the reality of the situation that one was born into or that developed due to environmental triggers (e.g., accidents, medical issues, etc.). These sessions can be valuable, as they provide support to assist the patient who is working through the past. This process can take some time. The full extent of our well-being is connected to our ability to take on the adversity we have faced, find healthy, proactive choices within our limitations, and make the personalized decisions to stay on the road towards happiness and success. This requires working through important points from previous chapters, namely, our automatic negative thoughts and the language that we use to deal with adversity.

Winter 2000-2001, 22 years old. I cannot believe I am speaking to my girlfriend's lover. A week or two ago, she told me in the parking lot of a Metro North train station that she was cheating on me. Although I left her that day, I return the next week to try to rekindle the relationship. Young and gullible, I rationalize through my Christian roots that I should forgive her. Interesting choice, looking back now.

Back at her home, she is in the shower and the phone rings. I answer it. It is her lover, asking pleasantly if he can speak to her.

Time stops. I have so many options here, but I am emotionally fragile. I plan to marry this girl because, at twenty-two, she is the first person, outside of my parents, who has told me she loves me. I think that means something. I still have poor ego strength and I miss the way she makes me feel loved and worthwhile. The very idea of our separation is like taking a blankie away from a three-year-old. The sense of emptiness is terrifying.

I resist conflict and ask this gentleman if I can take a message. I will regret this decision for the rest of my life. I take in his voice, wondering what he looks like, where he lives, what he has going on for him that made her choose him over me. I will learn that she became attracted to him when he washed her car at work. That makes me sick to my stomach. I learn that regardless of what one has accomplished on paper in terms of finances or degrees, relationships and sexuality are more complex than one can ever understand, especially at the age of twenty-two. I wonder if I can trust another person with my heart. I feel victimized for my goodwill towards her. It will take a lot of healing to date again.

New Year's Eve 1987, 8 years old. Do you believe that a single moment can alter the rest of your life, leading to experiences that do not make you proud of yourself?

I had never believed in the sliding door phenomenon. But, as I reflected after the phone call in my ex-girlfriend's apartment, my fear of being alone had all started when I was eight years old.

We have just moved back from Niagara Falls to Brooklyn. We are living with my grandparents in their apartment, decorated in classic style with furniture covered by thick plastic covering, the kind of place where you always ask yourself, *Why don't these people just take the plastic off?* It is New Year's Eve and my parents are going out with my aunt and uncle, so I will be staying with my cousin at their home that evening. Twenty-six years later, I still remember looking at my parents and telling them I do not want to sleep here tonight. I insist that when they drop my aunt and uncle off, even if I am sleeping, they have to wake me up and bring me back to my grandparents. I want to wake up the next day knowing that I am home.

My parents leave and the worst night of my life begins. I fall asleep. I am sure my eight-year-old brain, even while asleep, is still hyper-vigilantly waiting for that moment when I will awaken to see my mother's eyes telling me that it's time to go home and confirming for me that she is okay. My eyes open—but not because my folks woke me up. I look at the clock and it's 3am. My first thought is, *I am not home.*

I jump up. I run into my aunt's room and there she is with my uncle, asleep. My mind begins racing. I am asking questions. I attempt to wake them. I want to know how come my parents did not pick me up. Looking back, I am unclear if they were intoxicated, but knowing now what intoxication feels like and having experienced some New Year's Eves while intoxicated, I am sure they were not in the clearest mental state for dealing with my numerous questions at 3am.

I run to the phone. My plan is to call the house, wake my parents up, and demand to be picked up. I dial. Someone answers! It is my grandfather. I begin ranting,

NO MORE VICTIM MENTALITY: YOU CAN DO IT

"Grandpa, Grandpa, I need to speak to Dad. Please wake him up."

"John?" he asks. I say it again. My grandfather has passed away and I do not blame him or hold him truly accountable. But the next twenty seconds will forever ruin my childhood. The decision that my grandfather makes will alter the next nine years of my life. He says, "I will get him."

"Okay," I say. I feel great. But a minute goes by, and then another. No one comes to the phone. "That's strange," I say to myself. Quickly moving from enthusiasm to utter confusion, I hang up the phone and dial again. A busy signal. I dial again. Another busy signal. To my dying day, I will never know why my grandfather not only does not get my father, but also chooses to leave the phone off the hook.

I begin crying. I have lost sight of typical human behavior and spend the night cringing and pacing from one room to another, unable to tolerate this reality. I literally call my grandparents' place hundreds of times, constantly getting the busy signal. One day, I will learn in medical school that a significant amount of stress can alter the wiring of the brain. The next five to six hours literally undo the typical childhood that I could have enjoyed.

1987-1996. My nickname is "the shadow." No one really knows why as well as I do, but for the next nine years

I am incapable of not being near my parents. I will develop separation anxiety disorder.

In fifth grade, the principal announces that there is a tornado warning. I am flooded with irrational thoughts that the tornado will kill my parents. I freak out, reenact New Year's Eve from two years before, and cry until the teachers reach my parents. The next week, a lady will call me out of the classroom and conduct what I later realize is a therapy session. I tell her I am fine, which ends the therapy. Looking back, I wish I had stuck with it.

The following year, I am at my stepsister's house in Virginia for a family reunion. I am not told when my father goes to the store with my stepsister. Upon looking for my father and being told where he is, I cry in a room until he returns. I do this in front of the entire extended family.

The following summer, appreciating my early talent for basketball and hoping that immersing me in sports will relieve my anxiety, my parents place me in a summer sports camp that is intended to prepare me for high school basketball. Although I easily walk down the street from my home to play basketball, camp is at an unfamiliar location. On day one of the camp, not even an hour in, my mind goes to a dark place. I believe that because I am unfamiliar with this location, my parents will be too and they will not find me. I become frantic. A call is made to my parents to pick me up. Camp ends for little Johnny. I will not play high school basketball because of this incident.

NO MORE VICTIM MENTALITY: YOU CAN DO IT

In eighth grade, a female student throws a party at her home to celebrate graduating from middle school. My father tells me to go. I make it two blocks down the street before I become convinced my father will have a heart attack while I am away. I run home and miss the party. For all of high school, I will not go to a prom, a friend's house, or a party, and I will never go on a date.

I am seventeen years old and have not truly entered adolescence. I am a victim of my grandfather inadvertently hanging up on my eight-year-old self. It's very possible that I may have anxiety throughout most of my life. Whether I push through to experience some of life's wonders is up to me.

Fall 1988, 10 years old. "What do you mean this is your bike? This is my bike!" The tough street gangster kid pulls out his knife and puts it near my belly. He repeats, "Whose bike is it?"

"Yes, this is definitely your bike," I respond. But the worst part of being robbed at knifepoint when Craig and I are returning our movie to the local video store is that while this is happening, (1) a runner will run by who I think may stop my bike from being stolen, only to look down, see the knife, and casually run away and (2) after the thieves leave, we turn around to realize that the entire store—employees and customers—have watched this unwanted transaction occur from behind the safety of the store glass. Craig is pissed.

Summer 1991, 12 years old. I shoot a free throw, maybe the thirtieth of the 1000 that I have to shoot today. I look up and something across the street piques my interest. Time slows as my brain processes what I see.

My vision tells me there is a white guy wearing sunglasses, knees bent behind a car, *aiming a gun at me.*

My emotional cortex takes over and my thinking stops. And then the bullets come. I run and run for cover behind the handball courts. The run takes barely eight seconds, but those seconds are quite scary. As I turn around the corner to the court, a bullet hits the edge of the wall. Twenty-three years later, the chip in the court will still be there when I look for it. I stop running to look at the bullet. It's not a real bullet, but one from a BB gun. I am not sure about what damage I could have sustained, but these guns can easily pierce skin. Folks have lost eyes.

I run farther away. I will never tell anyone of this story, not even my parents. I never find out why this happened. It was probably one of the kids that I grew up with, messing with me. I make my way home. I think, *I have to succeed.* To get out of this area, I have to do better and work harder in school to make something of myself. I must learn to be resilient.

Fall 2001, 22 years old. Yeah, so, my bone is out of my arm. Man, I just did a sick crossover on the basketball court to this kid with whom I have been going at it the whole afternoon. He has scored on me, I on him, and maybe there has been some trash-talking going on.

Nearing mid-afternoon, I receive a pass from my teammate and decide I am going to the hole. I dribble left, crossover to the right and drive to the lane. As I take off into the air, my friend who has been guarding me pleasantly decides to take my legs out as a gesture of kindness. The ball leaves my hand. Realizing my body is now nearing horizontal as my legs have been taken out, I now have to extend my arms to brace for the fall on the wonderful solid concrete basketball court. I extend my arms and brace for the fall. As I land, all I think is, *Did the ball go in?*

I land. The other players, along with folks on the sidelines, yell out. At first it sounds to me like they appreciated the move I played on this guy and are giving me some positive feedback. I ask, "Did it go in?"

No answer. The players are still shrieking. I start to stand up, but this funny sensation comes over me. I don't feel my left arm. As I rise, I can see that it folds in half, floppy to the air. The bone is sticking out of my left wrist area. And yes, it is time to freak. I yell out to call an ambulance and off we go to the hospital, where it is confirmed that not just one bone broke in my wrist. Both bones have snapped, right in half. At this time I am temping in the city, still trying to make some money on the side in between acting jobs; my father is a salesman covering all of New York. With my dominant hand broken, I am temporarily out of commission and can't go to my job in Manhattan. My mother, a traffic cop stationed by day in downtown Manhattan, takes time off work to tend to me.

At this point, you would think this story is about the experience of seeing the bone coming out of my arm and the rehabilitation process of returning to normal life. But it's not. The day I break my arm is September 8, 2001. My surgery is September 10, 2001.

The day after my surgery, because of my broken arm, my mother and I stay home from our jobs in downtown Manhattan. My father leaves for an appointment at the World Trade Center at 9am, and an appointment in Queens in the afternoon. At 9am, however, my mother wakes me with the news: a plane has accidentally crashed in the World Trade Center. We don't know yet that the crash was a terrorist attack. "That's weird," I think. How can you miss those buildings? And then we remember that Dad was supposed to be there. We panic. Time passes, minute by minute. Just like that night on New Year's Eve many years ago, when I had my first panic attack and become known as "the shadow," I want more than anything to hear from my father.

He calls.

I don't know if you can attribute it to God or another higher power, but for some reason he switched his appointments and decided to go to Queens first. This chance decision, along with my trash-talking on the basketball court three days prior and a crossover that allowed this kid

NO MORE VICTIM MENTALITY: YOU CAN DO IT

to take my legs out and break my arm, possibly saved my family from tragedy. The two ladies at the World Trade Center that my father enjoyed doing business with, sadly, have died.

It is September 11, 2001. Everyone in New York is a victim today.

All of us are going to face some form of trauma in life. As I experienced the traumas in my own young life, the conclusion that always helped me was: "If I give in to this trauma today, then I cannot shape my life toward the goals I am seeking for tomorrow." My life was affected by terrorists, street thugs, and bullies, all looking to savor the fear I would emit as I emotionally curled up and crumbled. Over time, my reactions to trauma gradually became more limited, enabling me to become comfortable with dealing with "near misses" and close calls.

I became capable of moving past the emotional context of my experiences, so that I no longer allowed them to shape me—only, rather, to encourage me to use my mind to focus on what I could control and make the best of it. I found clarity in becoming a physician and helping others to work through their own stressors to become the best possible form of themselves.

I am pretty lucky that I continue, at least today, to be the best fully functional adult I can be. Even stating that I have experienced a lot for my time on this planet maintains some sense of victimization. It's always hard to let go of past traumas, but it is undeniable that my experiences *after* the bad times have shaped me more than the bad times themselves. I never allowed the bad memory of a cheating girlfriend to deter me from finding a companion in life. Sure, it took some time before I started looking again, but I never automatically concluded that all girls would cheat. Nor did I go into bars or on the Internet and loudly berate women as a group.

Because I developed intense separation anxiety from my father, I never stopped trying to expand on my life, hoping to generate a sense of autonomy and wholeness that would replace the security of knowing where my father was at all times. At some point, by trial and error, I was then able to grow and persevere to the point where I could travel the world alone and feel secure.

I didn't let knives, bullets, or even terrorist attacks shape my world and make it smaller so that I could feel safer. A person can easily shut himself in his home for safety, then slip in the bathtub and die from bleeding in the brain. We must push through our comfort zones. With a few detours, I ultimately was able to rise above the belief that the world was a scary place and that I should begin placing importance on violent and emotional traumas, letting them shape my personality and my life goals. I have trained myself to resist automatic reactions to traumas, which has allowed me to believe that life still can be a beautiful place full of joyous, wonderful experiences.

NO MORE VICTIM MENTALITY: YOU CAN DO IT

As I explained before, we all experience traumas in different sizes. To some extent, therefore, we are all victims. Once you recognize this fundamental premise, however, the key is to get yourself back to your previous baseline as quickly as possible, so that you continue striving, on your path, toward the same life goals as before.

You, the reader, have to look inside yourself and ask if you are fully working to return to your path. Are you allowing your traumas to shape you, or the other way around? How do you use your "language" to describe yourself to peers, relatives, and colleagues? Are you a victim, and thus still in recovery? Or are you rising above past victimization to return to your goals of becoming a lawyer, mother, or whatever your life dream is? The victim role impacts the larger obtainable goal. I promise you that the obtainable goal will bring you happier and richer experiences than the limited victim role.

In telling my personal story, I introduced the word "resiliency." The idea behind resiliency is to move past hardships and learn to make the best of the situation. I need you to practice developing resiliency to overcome the victim role. I would recommend starting today, with any time you experience a hardship. This hardship can be on the smallest scale—such as your partner, a family member, or even someone on the street doing something to you that you experienced as hurtful. Practice using your language mindfully. Do not allow yourself to say, "I cannot believe this bad thing that happened to me." Rather, begin saying,

"Wow, something bad just happened. I have to use my creativity to stay positive, focus on overcoming what I experienced as bad, and get right back to my task that I was working on." Implementing this change in thought and language in the context of smaller hardships will make it easier to be positive in the face of larger problems, as you will become more comfortable with focusing on the positive and preventing your negative feelings or self-image from seeping into your skin and sabotaging your future success.

Lastly, the better you become at not allowing victimized exchanges to affect you, the stronger you become as you move forward. Over time, you will notice that it takes more significant negative experiences to have a major impact on you. This improvement will free up even more positive brain usage that can be used toward future planning and preparation for your personal journey.

TAKEAWAY POINTS

- We all have been victims in our lives.

- The longer you fail to reach your potential because of your adoption of a "victim role," the less likely it becomes that you will actively place yourself in a position to seek that potential.

- Try to prevent a traumatic experience from shaping the way you define and describe yourself (a victimized person who "can't," versus a person who has been a victim and is now working on future goals).

- When smaller inconveniences happen, practice resisting the urge to use automatic thoughts and language to describe the experience. Exercising this discipline will minimize the negativity shaping your memory of the experience (and will assure an easier return to your previous goal).

- Practice resiliency. Make a game of demonstrating to yourself how well you can work through hardships and return to the active you.

CHAPTER EIGHT

CURIOUS LIKE A CAT

If you take a step back and look at life, sometimes it feels like we are hamsters on a wheel going 'round and 'round in circles. We wake up, go through the same routine, make the same coffee, take the same route to and from work, come home and watch the same TV program, and then drift off to sleep. For a person like me who enjoys discipline and time management, this sameness is comforting. However, when we look closer and examine our successes and our sense of happiness, there needs to be appreciated growth.

What does "appreciated growth" mean? How do we achieve that? Let's say you have a co-worker who at lunch on Monday asks, "Hey, what did you do this weekend?" You reply, "Oh, the usual. Went and saw my folks, visited a friend. Watched the Jets game." How would you feel about this weekend? Was it exciting? Was it boring?

As we mature, we look for experiences and folks who bring us comfort. We like life to be somewhat predictable, and less about excitement and adventure. If you are looking to reinvent yourself and grow, this habit can bring stagnation. In the chapter about friendships, you discovered that when you surround yourself with sluggish, inactive people, those familiar connections can consume so much time—and potentially introduce negative behavior into your life. This chapter discusses the opposite of familiarity and sameness, which is curiosity.

When we are children, there is a time when every aspect of life fascinates us to no end. We ask Mommy and Daddy what this is, what that is, and every why question in the book. However, as many of us grow into adulthood, that natural curiosity to learn everything about everything gradually disappears. Why does this happen? Why will many friends give me the stink eye if I ask for their companionship during a new experience? Examples include:

- Hey, I have free tickets to the ballet tonight.
- Hey, I am going to try that new Moroccan restaurant.
- Hey, I am going to try that free art class downtown.
- Hey, I am going to see that independent film.

Time and time again, as you mature you will be more likely to turn down an invitation to an activity because you have no interest in it, it makes you feel uncomfortable, or you have a negative preconception about it—in other words, because you are having automatic thoughts with an assumption about the idea. Perhaps your ego invalidates people who attend these events and thus cannot tolerate participating in them. In any event, your curiosity has dried up and blown away.

Because we have already discussed the negative aspects of how people lead their lives, in this portion of the book we will add the first *positive* aspect to your character. This aspect is about curiosity, beginning to take chances, saying "yes" to new experiences, and just closing your eyes and walking through the door even if you cannot see what is on the other side.

Folks who are negative use language to make assumptions about social experiences. They find no value in trying the new experience because they have lost their childhood curiosity. Somewhere along the journey of life, they created an internal sense of the world they feel they already know. This perception is absolutely not true. If you are confident that you can correctly anticipate all of your new experiences, your growth stagnates. Your development halts, undoing the journey to a successful and reinvented life.

When you are curious, life flourishes. Every single day can be an outlier. You have the power to undo the hamster wheel and fashion it into a go-cart, a diving board, or whatever you want it to be. I am not just referring to big plans to travel the world or buy a new car. I am suggesting that you consider checking out a different coffee shop, or reading the rival newspaper. Curiosity begins with small steps. By looking around, becoming mindful, and understanding why others seek pleasure from the less comforting experiences, you will experience growth on your own terms.

Life suddenly seems much more stimulating and thought-provoking when:

- A co-worker asks how your night was. Instead of saying, "I watched the ball game" for the one millionth time, you say, "It was a different kind of evening. I went to an art gallery exhibit for a change."
- Someone suggests, "Hey, want to head to the diner for lunch?" You reply, "Hey, let's go try that Vietnamese sandwich place instead."
- An old friend says, "Want to go shopping at the mall?" You reply, "Let's go to the reading by that famous poet."

These examples just increased your new understanding of the world three times over. You get to know what an art gallery opening is like: you met an artist, understood why he chose that form of art as his medium, and felt inspired by it. You ate a new type of food and can encourage others to try sandwiches from other cultures. Lastly, you listened to a poet recite her work in person and gained a newfound appreciation for her poems.

So instead of the ol' saying, "Same shit, different day," you are now the most interesting person in the room where you work. You have fascinating stories to tell and experiences to share because you have expanded your mind. Indeed, because you have grown, you become inspired to work on yourself further.

When potential patients call me, a common request for therapy is, "I feel stuck." The feeling of being "stuck" can operate in many domains. If you have developed symptoms of depression, your brain can actually become restricted in the biological sense. This phenomenon was once described to me as being comparable to someone placing blinders for racehorses over your eyes, so that your vision becomes restricted. This restriction impacts your visual ability to see more widely, so that both your thoughts and actions become increasingly more limited.

Anxiety, unlike depression, usually has a less acute onset: it is more likely to come on gradually over time, due to automatic thinking and a lack of exposure to new experiences. When a person narrows her world and what she exposes herself to, she is avoiding new experiences. As she becomes older, anxiety toward new situations and scenarios may increase. On many occasions, if the symptoms are severe enough, a medication can alleviate the symptoms. As all my patients know, if you work with Dr. Lops, there will be work required of you, primarily through exposure.

In my office, I complete a question-and-answer assessment to develop an appreciation for how strong my patient's curiosity muscles are. If narrowed and atrophied, this personality trait can often be a risk factor for depression, anxiety, and all-around dissatisfaction with life. I suggest that you review the chapters on negativity. Identify for yourself whether your thoughts, language, peers, and ego impact or limit the enhancement of your curiosity.

A twenty-seven-year-old woman once came to my office for anxiety and what we call "soft" depressive symptoms. She was new to the city and had assumed a new position in finance. Her peers were busy, and life was stressful. At times, she felt lonely. Although we worked on her thoughts and negativity to enhance her ability to tolerate her anxiety, her anxiety was not her only issue. When we discussed her issues around relationships, she revealed that to cope with her loneliness and the stress of her job, she found herself having random rendezvous with men she met at bars. These dalliances made her feel connected to another human and gave her a temporary sense of security, even for just one night. On the other hand, the encounters also made her feel guilty and self-critical afterwards. When her suitor left her apartment, she would feel worse and ashamed.

In our sessions together, we discussed why she had not considered online dating to be a more viable option. She had significant negative assumptions that she would never meet the right person. She also had an inflexible notion that humans were meant to meet potential companions at bars. I mentioned that in New York City, you are just as likely to meet the wrong person at a bar as online. We worked on shifting her automatic thoughts and undid her inflexible thinking. By the end of her session, she was curious about whom she might find online and how she could gain more control over her personal life—so that she could potentially meet someone who was genuinely interested in her, and not just a one-night stand.

A twenty-three-year-old man came to my office, referred to me through his family and friends. I noticed he was a quick-tempered and angry young man. He told me he wanted to work on controlling his emotions. When I asked how he currently controlled his emotions, his answer was marijuana. From a mental health point of view, this drug was a poor means of coping with negative emotions. But what else could he do? We did some exploring. From adolescence on, he felt as if people, including his parents, did not understand him. He therefore developed a negative belief that people never listened to him or appreciated him. Over time, his frustration led him to assume an angry persona when triggered. I was curious about what other methods he exposed himself to as a way of improving his ability to tolerate frustration. The answer: not too many.

As is the case with many of my patients, often some of the more straightforward therapy I do involves discussing a variety of activities that a client can engage in to undo stress and alleviate the unhealthy weight that negative emotions create. Finding healthy alternatives can undo this emotional and physical burden.

With my young, angry patient, we discussed the possibility of taking up boxing. Although he had never tried the sport, he had always been fascinated by boxers. He joined a gym, and over time integrated a healthy new exercise routine into his life that helped him to release his pent-up emotions. After work, if he felt that his emotions had been activated or triggered, he began acknowledging that he had control over his emotions and a healthy place to displace them. Additionally, the gym became a worthwhile social activity for him. He met like-minded folks who enjoyed the sport and he finally allowed himself to integrate his life with the lives of others. He even began going to other people's homes to watch fights on television.

Because all of his new peers were invested in their physical well-being, there were no triggers or temptations to use cannabis and his overall physical health improved. My patient drew upon his newfound curiosity to expose himself to a creative and positive means of coping with negative emotions. As a result, his life expanded exponentially, with improvements in both his physical health and his social life.

Curiosity was not my strongest personality trait as a youngster. I never left my father's side through adolescence, which drastically reduced my exposure to the kids I played basketball with down the street. My request for cucumber sandwiches for Thanksgiving dinner became a family joke. The first time my aunt took me to a ballet at age seventeen, I brought sunglasses because I planned to doze off. At that age, as soon as I heard the word *ballet*, I automatically thought, "Boring!"

By the time I reached college age, I had never had a conversation with a girl who could possibly enhance my social intelligence. I had never tried new foods, minimizing my likelihood of joining others to experiment with new restaurants. And I had never allowed myself to enjoy the arts because of the stigma that I, with my Brooklyn background, associated with ballets and operas. Is it any wonder that, during my freshman year of college, a girl asked me if I was suicidal!? I lived an extremely small, ignorant life.

One of the incredibly healthy life skills that my parents provided me with as a child was the ability to appreciate old Hollywood movies. My own passion for movies originated with my parents' passion for the oldies—from the original *Frankenstein* and *Dracula*, to the classics *Citizen Kane* and *Casablanca*. Unwittingly, my parents were also increasing my desire to be part of the movies. I remember the first time I asked my father how I might become an actor. He laughed and said, "Son, we are not rich enough for you to become an actor. Every famous person in Hollywood either came from money or their parents knew somebody who helped them." I had no retort. I was sixteen years old and had never met an actor or anyone who had ever had experience in the film world.

Three years later, while in college, I met a young lady to whom I enjoyed telling my tales of woe. She was Lucy to my Charlie Brown. Although she was aware that I was planning to apply to medical school after college, all I talked about, day in and day out, was acting. It was her healthy sense of curiosity that prompted her to ask me, "How come you never took an acting class?" I had no response. I just remembered what my father had said and told her that acting was for the rich.

The more we spoke about the possibility of my taking an acting class, the more curious I became and the more real it seemed. Then the day came to register for spring classes. Acting 101 was now on my schedule. And guess what!? I wasn't half bad. Then I wondered, "Hmmm…What if I audition for a show?" So for every semester until graduation, I took another acting class on top of my biochemistry classes. Furthermore, in each semester I was in a theatre production.

In my senior year, my acting teacher acknowledged that I lived in New York and thus had an advantage over many young folk, who must move away from their families to begin their acting careers. He said that if he were me, he would hold off on medical school and give acting a try. So I thought, "I wonder what being an actor would be like?" I called my father and told him I would not apply to medical school. He was incredibly disappointed, but he knew it was my life. From there it began, and I have had many wonderful professional experiences as an actor over the past fifteen years.

My capacity for wonderment has continued and grown, leading to an accumulation of wonderful experiences over the years. When Rock Band was the hype in 2008, my soon-to-be wife said, "Hey, for someone who never played an instrument, you are pretty good at playing drums in a video game." So, while in residency, I signed up for drum lessons. Five years later, I auditioned to be a drummer in a band and was accepted.

When my wife and I were to be married, she requested that we do an activity together to ensure that our relationship would grow. In the spring of 2012, she signed me up for the New York Road Runners, the local organization that endorses the New York City Marathon. Well, I considered myself an athletic guy and I loved playing sports, but running—wow. I had never enjoyed long distance running. After my first 10K (6.2 miles), I wondered whether I could, if I dedicated myself, train for the marathon. Eighteen months later, as we now know, the marathon was complete.

Throughout my life's journey, I recognized early on that no one could do the work for us. No one could make me an actor or make me a marathon runner. To get the benefit of increasing our life experiences, we have to be curious about how far we can take our lives. Curiosity truly makes life richer.

Life is what you make of it. People may say they like their lives. They like the routine of going to the same bar on Friday night, watching the same sporting event on Sunday, or taking the same route to work each morning. That is fine. For many people, however, I question if they truly like their routines. Is it possible that these routines, while not necessarily enjoyable, simply provide them with the most comfortable and anxiety-free experiences?

I have said this from time to time: humans like predictability. It provides a sense of comfort. I do not agree, however, that a predictable and comfortable life is necessarily a life full of growth. Would you watch a movie where the characters go through the same routine over and over? Life is living when you move out of your comfort zone.

The first step toward improving your curiosity is to identify if your choices in life are based on the comfort they provide. I am not saying that you have to take a different route to work every day —but if you had to, could you? Would the discomfort of the new route bother you? Or would the enthusiasm of the challenge spark your curiosity? That spark is what makes those special moments that break life's monotony.

I want you, on a weekly basis, to begin exploring life possibilities in your world. Start small, and be true to yourself. Begin by saying:

I wonder what it would be like to...

Again, start small. This exercise is not meant to flood your life. I am not asking you to wonder what it would be like to move to Bulgaria. Start with a new restaurant, coffee shop, gym, exercise routine, or art activity. Even smaller; be a little adventurous at the supermarket and buy a different type of fruit instead of your old favorite McIntosh apples. This type of exploration will stimulate many positive traits in you. It will advance your experience of life and create possibilities for meeting new people and networking, whether for social or professional reasons. You may learn something surprising about yourself, such as a new talent that you previously had no idea you had. Lastly, you will begin to tear down your inner walls, so that places of discomfort do not impact your decisions about participating in the world.

At some point—having acted for many years, attended medical school, and played the drums, for example—I ventured out of my comfort zone enough times to find that there is no inner sense of anxiety or insecurity that impairs my decisions about future experiences. If anyone suggests something that I have never done before, I want to see it and live something new. Even if an experience ends up being disappointing or not right for me, I have learned at least that I don't like it, and that is just as powerful—more powerful than just making the assumption that I would not like it. Actually engaging in a new experience, instead of just talking at the water cooler or bar about what you've heard second-hand from other people or your preconceived notions of what a place or activity might be like, will give your life a more profound connection to what is real and palpable. This change in living will then allow your mind, through curiosity, to request more of itself. Maybe, down the line, you will wonder what it's like to travel to South America, eat raw sea urchin at the new fusion seafood restaurant, or join a punk band after learning some new guitar chords.

Each time you begin a new challenge and you sense your mind resisting you, look back at the previous chapters. Are you making automatic assumptions? Are people around you trying to antagonize you for trying to improve your knowledge of the world? Are they supportive and empathic? Does your ego get in the way, so that you might feel, for example, that you are too cool to attend an art gallery? When you become more curious, you need to continue reverting back to the "negative" chapters earlier in this book, to keep your thoughts in check in case certain aspects of your outlook are impacting your ability to grow. Keep working on minimizing the negativity in your life as your curiosity develops. A virtuous cycle begins. You are cultivating your garden; life grows.

Once you begin having new experiences, use your language to share your enthusiasm and wonder. Sharing your new knowledge of the world will provide more sense of self than checking Facebook and obsessively wondering about what others are doing. That negative ego that had to go will evolve into something far better—a greater and deeper sense of self through further life experiences. And that is a wonderful thing.

TAKEAWAY POINTS

- Adults lose their childhood curiosity to avoid situations and scenarios that cause anxiety or seem foreign.
- Lack of curiosity creates a smaller world that prevents growth.
- Each week presents numerous opportunities all around us that will enhance our growth.
- Take risks and put yourself in new situations to meet new people and have new experiences. You will learn something new about yourself.
- It's better to have tried a new experience, and not like it, than to make assumptions about the experience. It makes you more interesting.

CHAPTER NINE

LET'S GO! YOU'RE GONNA BE LATE

Back in Chapter One, we discussed the negative assumption that you made when that pesky driver cut you off. Were you running late for work, or did you leave on time? When you woke up that morning, were you agitated because you set the snooze on the alarm, or because you had difficulty strategizing a route from the bathroom to the kitchen to the front door? Are you always texting friends that you will be five minutes late—and do they often get upset because you keep them waiting and waiting? Do you frequently underestimate the amount of time it takes to put yourself together to get to the movies on time?

If so, this is a sign of difficulty with the skill known as Time Management.

When you tell friends to be over at noon for lunch, do you get upset or anxious if they do not arrive until 12:10pm, or annoyed if they show up early at 11:50am? Do you experience an inner sensation of agitation when the smallest details are outside of your comfort zone? If you planned to go to a movie that is now sold out because your friend arrived ten minutes late, do you get thrown off-kilter when you have to revise your initial plan and see a different movie?

If so, your outlook may suffer from a lack of flexibility.

As you are preparing to leave for work, you tell your spouse, "Okay honey, when I go, I want you to upload those resumés online you promised me you would submit today. Today is a big day to start your new life!" Upon returning home, you find that he is hanging out on the couch, three episodes into the newest sci-fi show on cable. No resumés have been submitted, and once again you are disappointed. Your spouse may be struggling with what we psychiatrists call "task initiation."

Alternatively, perhaps the love of your life has successfully submitted her resumé and was called in for an interview, where the employer offered her an opportunity—a trial project, which your spouse must complete over the next three weeks. She is excited, and you're excited for her. She begins, but after a few days, she gradually begins to notice the project is a little harder than expected. A couple of nights later, you notice she is working less on the project and appears defeated. You inquire about the difficulty and ask what strategy she is using to overcome the challenges of her work. She stares at you blankly. She may have difficulty with "goal-directed persistence."

This chapter is about discovering ways to improve what are known as "executive functioning skills." These are the skills humans are blessed with to achieve higher-order success compared to our animal friends. Executive functioning skills, also known as "EFs," arise from a part of the brain called the prefrontal cortex. They are called skills because they are exactly that: they did not come prepackaged and programmed into your baby brain when you were born. We are all born with the ability to develop successful EF skills, but the ability to be on time, plan, organize, be flexible, stay attentive, start tasks, and complete them, despite distractions and other hurdles, are skills required for overall success in life, love, and work.

Yelling at a child, a loved one, or a colleague to be on time, start an endeavor, or finish a project on time will never change that person's ability to do it—unless that person is mindful of a deficit in a specific EF skill, and then develops the motivation and drive to improve it so that he or she functions better in life. Stories of people with EF skill deficits are all around us; such problems are frequently identified in children.

Parents often make the enormous mistake of assuming incorrectly that as children age and mature, they will automatically internalize EF skills—through some magical form of osmosis—over time. But parents, teachers, and other caretakers of children must create scenarios, provide support, and build incentives for children to develop these skills as they grow. Unfortunately, not every child masters these skills, and surprisingly many children become adults without EF skills. Without parents supervising their actions, it is much harder to provide an incentive for adults to improve these EF skills.

I hope that if you recognize your struggle with time management, flexibility, starting tasks, or completing tasks, you will continue forward—through experience, inspiration, and the motivation to reinvent yourself—to master an extra EF skill or two.

As a child psychiatrist, I frequently see attention deficit hyperactivity disorder (ADHD) in my office. ADHD impairs a person's ability to pay attention or sit still, which creates big dilemmas for teachers and parents trying to help children to improve their academic skill sets—specifically, EF skills necessary to structure their lives successfully. A child is generally classified as having the "inattentive" type of ADHD, the "hyperactivity" type, and/or the "combined" type.

For the last fifteen to twenty years, the gold standard for treatment of patients with ADHD has been a class of medications called stimulants. Commonly known stimulants include Ritalin and Adderall. With appropriate dosages and frequent assessments, these medications can be an incredibly effective treatment for patients with ADHD.

However, I have noticed a grave problem with this simple treatment: the medications do not magically improve a person's EF skills over the long run. This issue is evident in the adult patients in my private practice who were treated for ADHD as children or teens. These adult patients come to my office because they are suffering from anxiety, or because they are beating themselves up for having trouble with completing tasks, organizing, or making decisions to start projects.

What happened? These folks were on stimulants for ADHD as children, and I am sure that they were treated competently by good-hearted practitioners. I believe that the answer to the riddle is this: *taking a medication does not equal the practicing and mastery of a skill.* A medication does not improve our incorporation of a skill. Treating an ADHD patient with a medication, hoping it will somehow enhance the EF skills of this child or adult, is like eating protein bars or drinking protein shakes and waiting for the muscle to grow. The protein is the source of the nourishment that muscles need to grow after a workout, but it does not spontaneously cause muscle development on its own.

A stimulant decreases the severity of ADHD symptoms, so that the patient now has the ability to work on improving and gaining skills to organize, manage time, and plan, start, and finish tasks. The stimulants provide a helpful Band-Aid, but they're still a Band-Aid. You must practice these skills to get good at them, rather than just assume that a medication is the end-all, be-all panacea.

Not everyone who comes to my practice has ADHD. A thirty-four-year-old woman (with ADHD well controlled) came to me because she was experiencing depression. She recently had experienced high-stress events in her relationship. She was also struggling to find full-time work. Depression can lower effective EF skills. But even when her depression cleared, I noticed that she still struggled with her ability to follow routines in her life, such as getting up and going to sleep at regular times, starting tasks, and completing tasks. As I learned more, it appeared she had a high level of sensitivity to rejection. Why? Because her lifelong difficulties with EF skills, such as her inability to start tasks efficiently, had led to professional setbacks where she had been fired from full-time jobs and had not received positive feedback from her employers. As a result, she only took freelance jobs to pay her bills. Her sensitivity to the possibility of being rejected stemmed from the integration of her negative thoughts, automatic assumptions, and negative self-talk.

We developed a plan for my patient to restart learning good EF skills, so that, over time, she would undo the anxiety that came along with her fear of rejection. Although she is still freelancing, she has finally shown progress toward maintaining a daily routine: her sleeping patterns have become healthier, and her ability to work through difficult tasks successfully has improved.

In the years since starting my career as a psychiatrist, I have seen thousands of clients. I have noticed that with those people who seem to struggle with EF skills, there is a theme of feeling as if there is a "choice" in their lives.

These people believe they have options about even the most basic things:

- Should I go to work today or not?
- Should I pay the traffic ticket or not?
- I'm training for a marathon—should I run today or not?

This ambivalence is crippling for folks with deficient EF skills. During my marathon training, friends asked me how I could wake up at 7:00am on a Saturday and run for twenty miles. "Well, what do you mean?" I shot back, "There is no choice. There is no option. If I want to run a marathon, then I must train for it."

Of course, I'd love to sleep in. I'd rather watch movies, play video games, or surf the Internet. But if my goal is to run a marathon (as opposed to accumulating more hours of screen time), I had better drag myself out of bed and go run early on a Saturday morning.

Why can I do this? Why do I have this self-discipline? I believe it's due to my medical school experience. Medical school requires so many hours of hard work, discipline, and routine that if you don't complete what's required, you do not become a doctor. I have taken the skills I enhanced and developed over four years of medical school and continued to apply and re-apply them to different goals and objectives. I was not born with these skills, nor did I buy them at a store. They were nurtured through the support and encouragement of healthy role models, consistent dinners with my parents as a child, and an abiding interest in improving myself.

In the fall of 2008, I was thirty years old. When you ask psychiatrists which year of their training was the one in which they learned the most and worked the hardest, the majority will say their third year was the most challenging. The third year of residency is the clinical year where we actually begin to take care of our own clients: we are processing paperwork, managing administrative work, and seeing clients for the first time. They come to our offices with a wide spectrum of conditions and concerns. It is our duty, though early in our training, gradually to get to a point where we feel comfortable with our recommendations when our patients walk out the office door. In our training as therapists, this year is a big step forward. It's a difficult year.

Of course, I had to find more ways to make my third year of residency even more difficult. I took on a research project studying the early phases of bipolar disorder in youth. I also decided that I wanted to return to the stage and act, so I performed in three shows: the highlight that year was playing the title character in *The Elephant Man* at the prestigious Joyce Theatre in Manhattan. I am still asked to this day how I ever did it. The answer is simple. Over time, I truly mastered, and developed a broad range of, EF skills.

A sample day for me that year went like this:

- *6:30am:* Wake up and immediately visualize, or play out, my day in my mind. This exercise teaches you what is known as "positive anticipation." I am already seeing the day unfold in my head. I am feeling comfortable mentally and emotionally about what I expect, rather than taking each time slot as a potential surprise.
- *8:30am:* Arrive at work. Listen to voicemail messages and recreate a to-do list of what was not accomplished yesterday that needs to be added to today's list. This process is known as the practice of "task initiation," which helps to create my checklist of what needs to be done today. To help my brain to register emotionally which tasks are particularly important, I put a visual cue—a star—next to the high-priority items.
- *11:00am:* I receive a phone call from a client who requests to see me urgently. This client is not on my schedule for the day. I look at my schedule and make changes to accommodate his request, still ensuring that all my work is done before I need to head to rehearsal at the theatre. I never underestimate how long tasks take to complete. In fact, I generally overestimate so that when some tasks are finished earlier, I am rewarded with more time to complete other tasks. Not becoming emotionally affected by changes in plan allows for greater flexibility. I am

prepared for any nuances or shifts that may arise to affect the day I planned for myself.
- *1:00pm:* A client calls, asking me to call the pharmacy to refill a medication. There is no option. I complete the task and do not leave it for later or tomorrow. Just get it done quickly.
- *6:00pm:* Leave my office for rehearsal. Arrive at rehearsal at 7:30pm. In rehearsal, certain scenes for the show are not working. Our director provides me with redirection and notes. I am challenged by this, but I remain open to her interpretation and suggestions. She acts as a mentor to me and I keep myself available to her. We get through the scene successfully. With persistence, the scene is coming together.
- *11:00pm:* Drive back to home on Long Island. Go to bed at midnight and start the exact same routine all over again tomorrow.

Similar to training for a marathon, being the lead in a show, while simultaneously working as a medical resident, required the utmost expertise in EF skills. There were no options. I utilized all the tools discussed in this chapter, including time management, task initiation, flexibility, and goal-directed persistence. I did not allow frustration, upset emotions, or negative thinking to undo the process. Completing the marathon successfully in November of 2013 was one of the most exciting, cherished experiences of my life—right up there with my most challenging and rewarding acting roles.

Let's return to the fifty-pushup exercise. If you cannot do fifty pushups and you need to, it's simple: you practice. If you recognize you have a deficit in an executive functioning skill that is impacting your life, you have to practice that skill. Success depends on it; your happiness depends on it. The more of these skills you gradually master, the more efficiently you can eke out time to complete work projects, exercise, and—yes—even have fun.

Countless times, clients have told me about the various alarm clock tricks they use to get out of bed in the morning. Sure, they work, but the sentiment that's repeated when I speak to people who require alarms is that they truly wish they did not have to get out of bed in the first place. They genuinely enjoy the idea of sleeping and the sanctuary that their bed—representing the idea of sleep—brings. The bed is a safe place that does not supply negative emotions or negative thoughts.

This may sound cold, but a truly successful and inspirational man once said, "I'll have plenty of time to sleep when I'm dead." So true! Our bed, and the idea of sleeping, should not be a means for us to escape from life. Bed and sleep constitute a rest stop on the side of the road, solely needed for refueling and recharging. On a trip, the rest stops are not the highlights of our adventure. They are needed only for short intermittent periods to get our nourishment and gasoline for the car; daytime life, spent out of bed and awake, is the true adventure. Alter your mindset about how you view sleep, and you will start seeing it as a slight annoyance to living your life.

Next, if you really want a jolt to get the blood flowing after waking up and avoiding the snooze button, here's a tip for you. If you do not want to wait for the coffee to brew, just roll out of bed onto the floor and do ten pushups. The strain and intensity of the challenge will release enough adrenaline and endorphins to create almost instant mental alertness.

There are many things you can do to aid you with daily organization and planning. In my day job at the hospital, I am humble about how many daily requirements I can keep in my head. Being a visual learner, I always use a simple to-do list. One of my favorite tools to improve my to-do list is putting the highlighted letters, A, B, and C, next to each to-do item on the list. If you place an "A" next to an item, it means this task requires urgency and the highest priority. Over time, the A will create an emotional reaction to alert you that a task needs to be finished as soon as possible. Putting a "B" next to an item on your to-do list means that the task is not urgent. It needs to be completed, but you may have two or three days to complete it. Finally, labelling a task with a "C" means that you are aware of this task, but it can probably wait a week or so before it must be completed.

Every day, you update your to-do list. The A items are completed and disappear, the B items become A items, and so on. This simple system creates a visual style for organization and planning which adds an emotional aspect. If you have marker pens, you can use red markers for the A items to increase the emotional connection and the sense of urgency, yellow markers for B items, and green markers for C items.

Improving time management and flexibility requires discipline. I ask clients, when making plans, to allow more time and a larger window to complete tasks. For example, instead of telling friends or family they need to arrive for an event at noon, say they should arrive between 11:50am and 12:10pm. This approach teaches your brain to undo the obsessive, concrete nature of requiring people to arrive at an exact time and becoming upset when people do not follow your directions to the letter.

For your part, having an utterly nailed-down, specific timeframe for completion, and then inevitably failing to complete your task with exact precision and timing, sets you up to develop negative thoughts and emotions about how you implement and execute tasks. Increasing your window of time to complete a task or project will lead you to growing levels of success and confidence. Over time, as you improve, you can play a game with yourself: practice narrowing this window of time to enhance your mastery of your EF skills.

Finally, start small. If you struggle with EF skills, taking on too many tasks at once will naturally lead to disappointment and failure. Start with a smaller number of tasks to begin with and gradually increase the frequency of tasks, as well as the intensity and skill level required to complete the tasks. My time management skills allowed me to confidently be a physician by day and an actor by night.

As an initial goal, aim to have a solid month-long period where you wake up on time, get to work early, anticipate the day and successfully manage it, and go to the gym (or have dinner with your spouse or partner) when you come home. This practice will lead to more success in managing your time and getting things done; as a result, your EF skills will increase. You will naturally realize that you don't become as overwhelmed by time expectations. This discovery, which will enhance your confidence overall, may even lead to taking on another project or another hobby. You are mastering EF skills, which are the heart and core of all success in this world.

Do not live life looking forward solely to the rest stop.

TAKEAWAY POINTS

- Executive functioning (EF) skills are extremely valuable for success.

- Poor EF skills increase the risk for anxiety and depression in adults.

- When treated by medications, ADHD does not automatically improve EF skills.

- Working on EF skills is like training for a sport. You improve only to the extent that you make an honest effort.

- Using visual cues, exercise, anticipation, and flexibility about time will improve your EF skills.

- Improved EF skills lead to further goal-directed persistence because greater confidence in your ability to complete tasks is created.

CHAPTER TEN

THE POWER OF HUMILITY AND GREAT MENTORS

You are enjoying a nice dinner together with your spouse or partner. There's a gentle silence as you chew on good eats. A pause. Your senses are heightened. You tune in with your ears, and yes, you hear a steady *drip, drip, drip* coming from the kitchen sink. The same dripping sound you hoped would be gone by this evening. You look up at your better half and you know he'll be defensive, but you ask anyway. "Hey honey, I thought you were going to take care of the dripping from the sink."

He appears irked and replies, "I'll take care of it."

You hear him, but you ponder: if he was going to take care of it, well, why do you still hear that annoying sound? An agitated conversation ensues, in which you request that someone be hired to take care of it. Out of sheer frustration, he angrily responds, "I don't need a plumber! I told you I'll take care of it!" Two weeks later, the dripping noise remains the most familiar sound in your home.

Can you tell me, from the previous chapters presented in this book, which sections your spouse needs to work on in this case?

If you guessed he needs to work on "negative language" and "ego," you're correct. He knows he's struggling to fix the dripping noise, and because it makes him anxious when you answer, he reverts to hostile negative language to attempt to undo and end the questioning. Because you understand that using angry language to reply won't lead to a healthy, effective resolution, you don't reply. There's no need to create additional inner turmoil within yourself.

As for the procrastinating spouse who's left the kitchen faucet dripping for over two weeks now, he's struggling with his defiant ego. He also fails to appreciate and acknowledge that he doesn't possess perfect plumbing skills. Hence, he won't accept that others possess superior expertise, even if these "experts" have the capability to make our lives easier and more fulfilling.

This chapter is about the mentor and mentoring. Mentors are people in our world who carry expertise in fields we're interested in pursuing. They have the ability to not only download knowledge into our minds, but also to inspire us and motivate us to improve.

When we were growing up, in many cases, our parents served as our first mentors. They spoke to us, listened to us, and acknowledged and assisted us in areas we found difficult. In elementary school, our teachers became a source of inspiration. Their example motivated us to try extra hard to get that gold star for solving a math problem, and to push ourselves to go further.

In high school, we began moving away from adults and we began looking towards our peers for inspiration and motivation. Some teens, dedicated and seeking greatness, looked to those who had the discipline to excel at a sport, an art, or academic achievement. For others, looking up to peers became a source of darkness: it's often easy to be swayed by people who move away from pushing themselves, looking to find easier, more primitive means for realizing self-esteem. The kids on the corner, drugs, and sexuality became easy distractions from a disciplined routine and the development of healthy EF skills. These adolescents had no interest in guidance or support from parents, teachers, or coaches.

At some point, whether you master the developmental stage of adolescence or not, many of us will struggle to understand how we can further improve as adults. An old saying comes to mind: "There are only two types of people in the world. Those who ask for help from others and those who refuse to ask for help." The husband in the above example, who remains unable either to fix his indoor plumbing or ask for help, is an example of the latter.

Mentors are incredibly useful people. They can be found anywhere and everywhere. Mentors can be our loved ones, our friends, our teachers, our instructors, our sport heroes, and the folks we follow on Twitter or Facebook.

Mentors can assist us in developing passive inspiration, or they can have a specific active role in our lives. The human capacity to ask for—and accept—guidance, advice, and support from others is an incredibly positive trait to obtain and integrate into our personalities. Those who are not agreeable to the feedback of others struggle, developing a sense of frustration. This negativity will result in people becoming victims.

While many people recognize when they need the right person to help overcome a particular stressor, others are blind to the necessity of guidance from others. Why is that? As Chapter One states, our thoughts are not always our best friend. But, like the husband in our plumbing example, the people I'm discussing believe that their thoughts are *correct*: they are blind to the fact that their resistance causes a lack of growth (i.e., the dripping sink faucet not being fixed). This failing can create negative emotions and arguments as your frustration and impatience can disrupt your otherwise healthy relationship.

Mentors can help us to improve our abilities in the arts, sports, and the workplace; they can also guide us in honing our life skills. Sometimes we have to look out for the right mentor. We must be available to folks. Being open to their suggestions, having the ability to think outside the box, and reflecting on the skills mentors use can help you reflect on how you may have struggled to succeed in an area where you simply lack skills or expertise. Mentors can be amazing game changers. On our own, these opportunities can be few and far between.

Day after day, when I see various young boys shooting hoops with the little plush basketball in my Brooklyn office, I ask them, "Who's your role model?" To date, and it has been over three years since I began working at my clinic, the answer is almost always a sullen, "Nobody." I think back to the days when I watched basketball with my dad. He forced me to pay attention to Michael Jordan of the Chicago Bulls. He instructed me in the numerous skills Jordan used to develop his greatness at the game. Unfortunately, for most of the youngsters I help, they don't have a dad like I did. Even if the father is around, they don't watch television together: invariably, the father is preoccupied with his favorite show and the kid plays independently on his smartphone or tablet.

A thirty-two-year-old man came to my office. He complained of feeling stuck and frustrated with life. He worked in a retail store. He told me that school wasn't his thing; he liked being around people, and sales positions were the employment opportunities that felt right to him. However, as he matured, he grew increasingly frustrated with these lower-level positions. Indeed, most of the people in his life—his parents, other family members, and friends—strongly encouraged him to return to school, move up the chain of command at his current job, or learn another trade that could provide higher pay (or at least some semblance of benefits). What was going on here? I learned he never had parental figures who inspired him when he was younger: his parents, focused on their own careers, hadn't "checked in" to see how their son was developing, and had spent little vital time with him as a child on working to enhance his skills. It was only later, when they realized that their son had plateaued as an adult, that his parents showed a sense of urgency about his life direction. He developed poor self-esteem due to his difficulty with academics, and he would accept positions that minimized his anxiety and paid his bills.

In itself, his desire to hold down a job and pay his bills was fine, but his comfort zone was his downfall. Never having sought to improve internally, he stopped growing as an adult and neglected helpful, well-intended advice from others. Everyone else saw it coming, sensing that he would gradually become frustrated in his adult life and at some point would want more, but he refused to allow others to assist him in moving beyond his comfort zone. As I mentioned before, living occurs when we move past our comfort zone. It took my patient ten years of sales positions until he realized his choice of career was not sustainable over the long term.

Together, through therapy, we created a safe place in which to discuss possible risks, gain more confidence, and undo his fragile ego. We unwound the negative thoughts that had prevented him from believing that if he tried, he could successfully move on from retail jobs. In this situation, I became his mentor: he opened himself up to me, agreeing to consider another person's advice and feedback. My patient now works for the city and has exciting options for growth in his career. He receives medical insurance benefits, and he will receive a pension when he retires.

A thirty-six-year-old man came to his session with me. In contrast to the gentleman described above, this man was quite successful in his career. As the owner of a business that he had built up from scratch, he did well financially and was proud of "making it in New York City." He eventually married and spoke highly of his wife, who also seemed lovely and engaging. He came to see me because something in their marital relationship was causing him frustration, making him act irritably towards her. His wife asked him to see someone to discuss his feelings.

At the heart of my patient's problem was an inability to incorporate his wife's suggestions. He appreciated that in business, he'd always followed his own lead and listened to his instincts—with stellar results. Success in relationships, however, is more complicated than following your instincts and gut reactions. Relationship success requires open dialogue, and what I call "allowing the other to affect you." In other words, it requires humility—because relationships are about the team. Even when one partner "wins" a dispute, he or she will both share in the frustration endured by the "loser." If one half of a couple focuses on "winning" in a relationship, both people in the relationship have lost.

In our sessions together, my patient and I explored the development of the humble ego. We looked at the importance of letting go of the feeling that he was always "right," and learned that in a successful relationship, both parties must feel validated for long-term success. Victory in relationships is achieved when one person successfully accepts the influence of the other. Accepting this influence can mean taking on a new sport, dabbling in art, or partaking of cultural experiences; broadly stated, it means allowing someone else's life experience to affect our growth, just as we would accept a mentor's guidance. In our sessions, my client was gradually able to become more aware of the times when he was rejecting his wife's suggestions, and to actively tell his mind to be open to her thoughts and ideas. Over time, with progressively less effort, he became more capable of desensitizing himself to his automatic negative thoughts about accepting his wife's input. The relationship became more positive for both of them as his newfound ability to incorporate his wife's suggestions became more natural. In a manner of speaking, if there were a dripping noise in the kitchen, he would have called the plumber.

Spring 1998, 19 years old. It just wasn't working out. I was not seeing where it was going wrong socially, especially with women. Then a friend of mine finally summoned up the nerve to ask me, "Dude, what's with all the sweaters and sweatpants?"

I didn't understand what he meant at first. I was following the fashion trends I thought were cool: I wore shirts that represented my favorite sports teams. But my friend clued me in on a little secret. Girls would not date me for my athletic apparel. He brought me into his dorm room, asked me to remove my Notre Dame sweatshirt, and went to his closet. He pulled out a button-down shirt, nothing that appeared opulent to the naked eye. Like a fine Italian tailor, he placed the shirt on my body. It gave me chills. I buttoned it up and he walked me over to the mirror.

At that moment, life changed for me forever. I had donned my first Tommy Hilfiger shirt. My mind spun. My eyes burned. It was like I saw a new world for the first time. I was reborn.

Suddenly my sweaters and sweatpants looked horrible. I had learned what fashion was and I wanted to know all about it. Two months later, one of my nicknames at school was "Perry Ellis" because of my appreciation of fine clothing.

My friend mentored me to improve my sartorial sense. Up until that moment, I was blind to what people wore. To this day, I still love and appreciate fashion. If I hadn't been curious about my friend's taste in clothes and allowed him to mentor me about designer labels, I might still be wearing purple sweatpants with a Lakers logo riding down the side of my arm.

Spring 2005, 26 years old. In the middle of my fourth year of medical school, in an effort to enhance my resumé for my residency interviews, I decided to take an elective in research to become a little more well-rounded. When I contacted a local hospital and scanned the available options, an elective in neuroimaging—which would mean working with a researcher who studied MRIs to learn more about mental illness—caught my eye. I applied for the elective and got it. A week before the elective was to begin, however, the director of medical student electives called to inform me that the researcher had become ill. The elective was cancelled.

As the director scrambled to find another elective on the outline for me, she began to tell me about another researcher: someone who was young, had a lot of energy, and would be a "good fit" for me. I replied, "Sure." The decision, made on the spur of the moment, would have a lasting impact on my life. Jadrian became my research mentor. I ended up working with him for the next six years, learning so much more about research and protocols than I ever imagined. It was his guidance that allowed me the opportunity to become published in a medical journal for the first time.

Research is a daunting endeavor and one that requires a highly disciplined personality; I eventually became

THE POWER OF HUMILITY AND GREAT MENTORS

burned out from it as I entered my fellowship in child and adolescent psychiatry, and I began to think of other opportunities. Chris, my next mentor as well as my training director, began discussing roles within my employer's national organization. For the next three years, due to my research background and enthusiasm, I was extremely fortunate to have leadership roles within the organization in which I developed lectures and panels at well-recognized institutes.

During my last year of training, each of us had to choose a supervisor who worked in the community. I picked Charlie because he had good business sense and because he understood how health care and policy worked together. It was a wonderful year full of learning and growing. I was able to pick his brain about opening up a private practice. His advice helped me to begin learning about how to run what was, on many levels, my own small business.

By 2011, I had experienced amazing mentorship from three experienced professionals. I had also gained familiarity with a multitude of fields in the practice of psychiatry that not every medical student or resident experiences. My curiosity and hard work took me on a ride that involved working intimately with folks who actively changed my field, whether it was through research, policy, or clinical practice. I thank all three of them from the bottom of my heart for acknowledging my interest in their mentorship and bringing me into their worlds—so that, as I grew, I could decide based on the truth, not the "what ifs," on the kind of psychiatrist I wanted to become.

I was about twenty-three years old when I had my first significant adolescent rebellion against my parents. Late, I know. I was frustrated by my parents' limitations in assisting my acting career. My unhealthy narcissism ran rampant. So many folks had told me that I would make it as an actor and felt my passion and talent, but I felt that my lack of connections was holding me back. I found the easiest folks on which to project my anger: my parents. Irritable that the lives of my blue-collar parents did not allow them to accumulate the social capital necessary for me to achieve my ideal of fame, I regrettably caused a stir. I made ridiculous comments about wishing that I was born to another family that knew people in the industry.

In retrospect, my behavior was just ridiculous. Granted, my parents were not the most social people, but it never prevented me from recognizing that others were available to help. While I did not become a famous working actor, I ultimately realized that I was casting myself as a victim of my upbringing to make excuses for why I wasn't growing personally or professionally.

The first recommendation of this chapter is to step back and recognize how you can participate in improving your mentorship connections. I don't mean "connections" in the social media sense: sites such as LinkedIn are solely means to find new work opportunities, not to enhance our personal growth. Rather, I ask you to look within your immediate connections, take a step back, and think about what they can offer in terms of advice or feedback. Maybe there is Bob, the older gentleman who works in the tiny office down the hall. Bob has been at the company for ten years; you've only been around for two. I am sure there are plenty of questions you can come up with that Bob can answer—along with some pithy insights and sound advice.

Folks get trapped into focusing only on those direct connections that lead to promotions and pay raises. I think that's a mistake. I suggest you look at anyone who has a year more than you in experience—be it experience with an employer, a professional field, dating, or investing. We should be using the folks around us for their stories and their wisdom as we try to understand why they have made the decisions they have made. I promise you that the more you understand the simple life decisions that your fellow man or woman has made, the more useful information you have with which to find your own path.

One of the greatest and most memorable moments of mentorship I ever received was simply from a friend over dinner. She herself was a physician; at the time, I was about to begin residency. When I asked for her advice, she said, "Johnny, whatever you do, when you get home from a day at work, don't sit down and watch TV. Drop your bags and plan something for the night." That was it. *Simple.* And that one line stuck with me so poignantly for the whole of my residency—as I completed extensive training at an improv school, toured with an improv group for a year, and performed in three plays. A brief moment of guidance was all it took for me to realize that I would hate my life as a resident if all I did was work, go home, vegetate for a little, sleep, and go back to the hospital. Her one line inspired me to create experiences in residency of which I am very proud.

If mentorship and guidance only came from the folk who could make me famous, I would still be waiting for such a person today. *Mentors are everywhere.* We just have to be humble, available, and willing to ask for their time. In that time, we can ask our mentors questions to help us understand their experiences—and allow them to know just a little about us, so that they might share some insights into how we should move forward.

I am constantly amazed that even in my work, and especially in my work with the kids, how seldom patients have asked me what I think they should do going forward. And, as this book shows, I've seen a lot. But they won't ask. Humans sometimes are too uncomfortable to ask for help from others. We do not want to put ourselves in the subordinate position. In this world of selfies and reality TV, it's all about me and everyone should want to know what I do. Unfortunately, however, we all hit the limits of our knowledge. Growth requires input through experience; others may have the experience that we lack.

Being available for my friend to put that first Tommy Hilfiger shirt on me was a game changer. My newfound confidence would help me in medical school, where I had more conventional mentorship relationships with very experienced and admired people who taught me the skills I would need to succeed as a professional. In some ways, however, my path really started when I was just a kid who wanted to be cooler and cuter to girls. My friend's pointers about something as mundane as shirts was a defining moment in my life—not only because it changed the way I dressed, but because it was a moment when I realized that opening my mind to the advice of others could help me improve my life. My innocence and curiosity, which are prerequisites for finding good mentors and enjoying the wonderful life experiences that may come from their guidance, have never left me.

If you find yourself arguing with others any time guidance is provided or you think Bob is a loser and that's why he has been down the hall at his tiny office for so many years, you need to go back and read the chapters on automatic thoughts and ego. Without asking Bob his story, you are only making assumptions. Without asking Bob, you are missing a wonderful opportunity to learn from someone's experiences in your industry. Go find your Bob!

REINVENT YOURSELF: ESSENTIAL TOOLS

> **TAKEAWAY POINTS**
>
> - Actively seeking out mentors is a key component of success.
>
> - Mentors do not have to be rich or famous people! A mentor can be anyone who has one more day of experience than we do in any area of life.
>
> - Open-mindedness, and the willingness to try new behaviors or thoughts different from your own, are crucial to getting any benefits from mentorship.
>
> - Mentorship can be a suggestion, a brief encounter, or a recommendation from someone else. It does not have to mean long-term guidance.

CHAPTER ELEVEN

WHAT DID YOU SAY: THE ART OF ACTIVE LISTENING

Tonight it's Friday. You are meeting that new guy from an online dating site. Your outfit is carefully chosen, your friends say you look awesome, and out the door you go.

He is waiting for you at the bar. Your first instinct is that he looks cute, and you head over to a table to enjoy dinner together. After a few minutes, though, you begin to suspect trouble. You try to begin telling him about your workplace and your job—but each time you finish a breath, he replies with an "Uh-huh" or "Yep" before shifting the conversation back to talking about *his* job, accomplishments and interests. When you share that you're having a difficult time with your parents, he glumly replies, "Oh, that sucks." You notice yourself becoming irritated. In an attempt to redirect the conversation, you say that you recently began volunteering at a youth center. He almost laughs and shouts out, "Why?"

Anger sinks in as you realize this guy is making no effort to develop the chemistry you were seeking in a partner. As you try to calm yourself and discuss the latest movie you saw last weekend, you notice he is distracted: his eyes are glancing furtively around the bar. Finally, you go back to discussing something you both know about—your jobs in the world of finance. He talks about how well he is doing, and you respond by sharing some of the difficult bosses you have worked with. As soon as the conversation shifts away from his own life, though, he loses interest. "You should just quit," he responds with finality.

That's it! You have had enough. The check comes, and thank goodness he at least pays the tab. He walks you to a cab, and as you say goodbye, he tries to give you a kiss. You are taken aback and pull away from his efforts at affection. He is embarrassed and confused. The man is surprised when you text him later that he was nice, but it's simply not going to work out.

When one party fails to practice the mindful art of active listening, common social interactions such as dating can become downright painful for all concerned. This chapter is focused on particular aspects of our daily lives where active listening can improve our experiences with relationships and work.

In the above example, how did our gentleman friend contribute to this dating disaster? In the early part of the date, he was just "yepping" our heroine each time she tried to share some aspect of her life. His almost monosyllabic replies and lack of conversation and healthy feedback caused her to feel that he was not listening and that he was invalidating her. He never acknowledged that he even heard what she said. Later, she opened up about her parents and was hoping for some empathy about how difficult it can be with our parents as they grow older. His two-word response ("That sucks") undid all her efforts to appreciate his emotional side.

His strategy made it impossible for his date to continue sharing her problems regarding her parents. He dug himself into a deeper hole by following up with a sarcastic "Why?" when she spoke about beginning to volunteer, which made her feel defensive and judged—not the best strategy for setting a romantic, inviting mood on a first date. Finally, he tried to make her feel better about her work and her challenges with her boss when, in an effort to offer his best version of sophisticated advice, he told her that she should just quit her job. He was well-intentioned, but this kind of preaching is not the kind of response you want in a potential partner. Are you surprised the woman in this example developed no interest in, or attraction to, our fellow with severely poor communication skills?

Dating and sexuality are at the forefront of some of the most difficult aspects of communication. Supportive, kind, and genuinely interested forms of listening—verbal and non-verbal—can ensure that both people are on the same page. Most folks who struggle with dating and friendships show difficulty with active listening skills. Sometimes you can get so nervous that your brain cannot even process when you are supposed simply to be silent and listen to what the other person is trying to communicate. Anxiety and anger can cause your speech to be pressured; your mind races for the next smart thing to say as you listen only for the other person's indication you are right. Indeed, when many people are not told they are correct, they become more angry and less tolerable to be around.

Active listening requires many processes to occur all at once. It requires you to listen well and to make the other person acknowledge you are listening well. It also requires an absence of unhealthy social cues that can inflict frustration on the other person. Lastly, it requires learning how to ask non-selfish, relevant, and interesting questions to ensure that a good conversational flow continues, free of negative emotions.

A continued connection also requires significant non-verbal skills. In the example described above, when the long-suffering heroine tried to switch the conversation to something simple like movies, she noticed that the man was not even making eye contact—another simple mistake. Making eye contact is the first step toward creating the most basic of relationships. At any bar, workplace, or social situation, if you are not making eye contact with the speaker, she will not consider you to be interested.

Moreover, our brains are highly wired to look for non-verbal cues in our conversations, thus allowing for a healthy ping-pong effect to occur: we both know who wants to speak and when it is time for the other to speak. Another cue is a simple nod during pivotal parts of the conversation. The nod tells the other person, "I got you," and signals that the speaker can continue. After a few more nods and statements, it's usually the listener's turn to begin speaking instead.

If we are truly to stay interested in each other, to be curious about the experiences of others, and to develop fulfilling, reciprocal relationships that are more than just "What have you done for me lately?", then active listening skills are a crucial aspect of success and long-term happiness.

My field provides me with extensive daily exposure to strains in relationships that arise from poor listening and communication skills. As a child psychiatrist, a large portion of my job involves detecting when and how communication has gone astray within families. Some of the most severe presentations to my office are related to the difficulties that young people have in communicating with their loved ones, and vice versa.

In particular, one of the most challenging presentations to my office involves a kid, generally a teenager, who presents with self-injurious behaviors. Most presentations are in the form of cutting. Cutting is a complicated presentation for us physicians because it is quite difficult to simply find alternate means for the child to self-soothe during periods of stress. In my experience, a majority of kids who cut use this behavior because, as children with limited control in the household, they find no other means to have control. Simply put, they feel that they are not being heard and find that their parents are not available to them for communication.

Although the children complain of having no voice, it is not uncommon that the parents themselves have provided what appears to be adequate availability and dialogue. The child nonetheless yearns for more than can be accommodated. When pushed, teenagers will use difficult behaviors, such as cutting or common oppositional behaviors, to communicate their fractured mental state. It is my job to improve healthy means of communication while lessening the child's need to use these more pathological modes of communication.

Another difficult presentation to a child psychiatrist's office, which also fundamentally arises as a result of minimal dialogue between kids and their families, is eating disorders. Anorexia nervosa is a very difficult and deadly disorder in our field. In my practice, anorexia tends to have its roots in fractured communication within family units. The child uses weight loss as a means to gain control within the family; a high level of investment in sports and academics is relatively common. When the family begins to appreciate that a medical ailment is coming upon the child, the discovery ignites a severe conflict between the parties, demonstrating communication at its worst. Parents threaten, children cry and act out further, and the family unit becomes increasingly undermined with each passing week; the marriage of the parents is typically pushed to the brink of sustainability. Crucial to the treatment of anorexia are separate, parallel sessions with both child and parents. Improving healthy dialogue between all parties, as well as encouraging support and understanding, form the foundation of the best long-term prognosis.

Self-injurious behaviors, oppositionality, and eating disorders are some of the most severe cases I see. A recurring thread in these cases is the struggle for healthy communication *between* parents. For example, a mother came to my office to discuss her young daughter. We were having a pleasant conversation in which I discussed my thoughts about the daughter's case. At the time, the mother's emotions were stable; she was engaged in the discussion and focused on what I was saying. Then the phone rang and she looked down.

For me, time slowed. I could see her brow change angles and her body tense. "WHAT?!" she answered, "I am at the doctor's office. I can't talk." With little time for whoever was the victim of that call, she hung up. I inquire who this was that induced such fury. She responded, "My husband."

I asked the mother of my patient, "Do you realize what just happened?" She looked perplexed. I explained that I had noticed drastic changes in her physical attitude and verbal tone as she saw who was on the phone. Upon further discussion, I came to understand that lines of communication with her husband had gone sour, to the point where she now automatically used very negative and hostile means to communicate with him. I calmly told her that her daughter's well-being would never improve if we did not start with communication between the mother and her husband. Poor communication is like genetics: it gets passed down if children learn by example that yelling and screaming are the best tools for getting what you want in a conversation.

Whether it's the first date, marriage, or raising a healthy family unit, it all begins with ensuring that we have the tools to be active listeners. These tools are utilized to overcome a majority of life's most difficult stressors, and play a key role in treating some of the most challenging psychiatric conditions I see. Taking the time to enhance these skills is of the utmost importance.

Spring 1998, 19 years old. As a budding psychiatrist, my active listening skills were among my strong attributes. In my youth, however, the listening skills necessary to understand the opposite sex were laughably absent.

By sophomore year, my sadness from a lack of healthy dating was so severe that people were expressing concern that I would hurt myself; my mentor across the hall had even volunteered to improve my fashion sense. Despite my despair, however, some girls were beginning to show interest. This semester, Allison was spending more time in my friend's dorm room. Each time I entered, her eyes widened with euphoria. Each day I came home from class and looked forward to seeing a girl who made eye contact with me longer than the typical gal. I would sit on the floor while she perched on the bed and tussled my long, early Brad Pitt hair as we laughed and talked. Sadly, my mind could process none of these signals. All of her non-verbal cues went in one ear and out the other.

On one eventful night, my friend invited me out to our local college bar. Until this night, I had never gone out off-campus before. Just minutes after we got to the bar, lo and behold: who was there, dancing alone, but Allison! I walked up to her, said hi, and we began dancing. Of course, I interpreted the glazed look in her eyes as too much alcohol. It never occurred to me that a beautiful lady like her would be interested in me. None of the cues—not the wide eyes, not the playing with my hair—affected me: I had accepted my fate as a boy in whom no girl would ever be interested. We danced and while we spun, my guy friends would spin with us, making subtle playful gestures behind her. I laughed.

As the end of the night approached, my friend offered to drive Allison and me back to our dorm. Being a gentleman, I opened the rear door for Allison, but my friend, being a solid guy, shoved me back there as well. She laid my head in her lap and played with my hair; oblivious, I thought about what time I needed to get up to start my organic chemistry homework. We parked and entered our dorm, walking the one flight of stairs to our hall. In this particular dorm, there was an intersection of two corridors, with the girls' dorms to the left and us fellas to the right.

Time slowed. Neurons were beginning to fire about some possibility, gleaned from the accumulative interactions Allison and I had had, that something might happen. But the lifelong feelings of self-defeat took over. We got to the intersection demarcating the girls' dorms and the guys' dorms, where Allison and my friend took three steps to their respective halls—then stopped and looked at me.

I stood at the intersection, frozen in indecision. I looked at Allison and she remained wide-eyed, beautiful as always. I looked back at my friend, who with such good intentions was gesturing for me to go the other way. I looked back and forth multiple times. I took in a breath and exhaled, "Well, good night, Allison," and walked towards my friend. Defeated, I asked, "What's up? You think she liked me?"

He grabbed me by the shoulders and slammed me against the wall. "You moron!" he shouted. He took me by the collar and walked back down the other hallway. He stopped at her door and knocked. "Come in," we heard.

My friend opened the door and said, "I have a delivery for you." The door closed. And there I was—definitely a change from my typical routine of watching *The Tonight Show* with my roommate.

I was a great verbal listener, but clearly one of the worst non-verbal listeners of all time! I had learned some skills that night—skills needed to move forward with my social life and assist in finding a partner.

Active listening skills are crucially important tools. In my work, I have found that many conflicts arise, at focal points of our lives, through an absence of matured listening skills. These conflicts can fracture relationships between parents, between parents and kids, between work colleagues, and even between you and the person working at the DMV!

Let's look at steps to improve your listening. You and I are at a coffee shop, our coffees in our hands. We have not seen each other in some time. The first and best recommendation to ensure a positive interaction is the eye contact. It's that simple; anything less, on the other hand, will impact all forms of communication. Appearing distracted by looking at your phone or your watch, or showing curiosity in anything more than what we are saying to each other, is a major pitfall.

You ask about my work and I begin to discuss some of my challenging cases. Now, if you are just staring at me while speaking, it would look odd; I might think you are possessed. So we need to start adding some gestures to show that you got me and are making sense of my words. Simple gestures such as "I gotcha," "And then?", or "That makes sense" inform me that you are rolling with my words. As stated early in the chapter, the non-verbal nod at pivotal points in the conversation informs me you are listening.

As my stories become more informative and as I share more personal details, other responses are used to create further cohesion between us, two coffee-drinking friends. Occasionally, when I tell you about a challenging experience, a simple "That seems hard" would enhance our dynamic. If I say something cool or positive, "That sounds awesome!" would really show you are enjoying my story.

Now that I have shared some stories or personal experiences, I, the speaker, want to confirm that you really understood and internalized my message. How can you do that? Simple. Through subtle gestures such as rephrasing or summarizing what I just said. If, in the midst of a difficult story at the hospital, you add, "It seems like work there has become harder," or "I think I am hearing your patients are becoming more difficult," your response tells me that you understand my day-to-day problems.

At this point, I have spoken for some time. It would be easy and appropriate for you to begin sharing *your* story. But, alas, there is one more tool here that will enhance my appreciation of your friendship. A nice "What are you going to do about work?" provides an open-ended question which provides me the chance to think in the moment, while showing me that you are interested. Given these cues, I can now respond with a "What do you think I should do?" that validates the importance of our friendship.

Open-ended questions are a sign that you are interested in what the other person is saying and give that other person significant freedom within the conversation. Such questions are quite useful for friends whom we have not seen in some time, people we are getting to know on dates, and other important folks in our lives. It shows curiosity about the other person. Here are some examples of questions that allow for expansive conversation to occur, enhance our interest in others, and display more skills to show off how amazing a listener we have become.

- How are you?
- Where have you traveled in the past?
- Where are you from?
- Who do you know at this party?

In my world, another skill that facilitates the improvement of a working relationship is commenting on another person's "affect." Your affect is your emotional expression when communicating. Going back to my example where we are at the coffee shop and I am discussing my difficulty at work, a great tool to show that you appreciate my difficulty would be to comment, at a certain point, on how I appear externally. Telling me, "You look so upset" confirms to me that you appreciate the complexity of my feelings towards my job. This gesture isn't just about humans and words; it's about our feelings, and it's about showing that we care about each other past the surface.

Think about all the other places where commenting on someone's affect can be an appropriate gesture. Suppose that your husband comes home from a tough day at the office or your sister calls to talk about some difficulties with her marriage. Statements like "Honey, you look so tired" or "Hey sis, you sound upset" provide non-direct but highly appreciated dialogue, spurring a level of attachment between two people that moves beyond simple words.

Lastly, let's return to our poor friend at the beginning of the chapter—the guy who struggled on his date due to several communication no-nos. His sarcastic "Why?" and "You shouldn't" represent non-empathetic language. Other statements, along the lines of "Stop worrying about that" or "Just do it then," can be seen as hostile and unsupportive.

This chapter has looked at a multitude of healthy means to ensure good, supportive communication. Think about these strategies and practice them in your world. Active listening helps to remove negative thinking from your mind and minimize negative interactions between people. Lessening negativity will allow more room for healthy and easier life experiences, thus enhancing your journey towards success and happiness.

TAKEAWAY POINTS

- Active listening is vital to healthy and successful communication between people.
- Listening skills need to be practiced and can be progressively improved.
- Open-ended questions display your curiosity towards others.
- Rephrasing and summarizing are simple ways to show that you listened to important points in the stories that others tell.
- Non-verbal tools, like good eye contact and nodding, show you are paying attention.
- Commenting on the affect of the speaker strengthens your connection with the speaker in a way that goes beyond simple words.

CHAPTER TWELVE

HOMAGE TO MY DAD: KILL 'EM WITH KINDNESS

After a flurry of interviews and second visits, you've finally received the call: Corporate wants to hire you. You accept the position, appreciating that the money seems good and that the job is a step up in your profession with good benefits. Your future colleagues, especially your future boss, seem so nice—they're so pleasant and agreeable! When friends ask you about your new position and why you chose it, you acknowledge that other potential employers offered you a similar salary and comparable benefits, but the job starting today was the right choice based on the vibe of the working environment. It just felt right to you.

Monday morning comes. The new job awaits you, along with new opportunities, a new office, and new co-workers. Your first day begins and everyone is smiling, asking questions about you and promising to assist you as you learn the ropes.

Two weeks later, your first project is not going as smoothly as you expected. You recognize that certain programs are unfamiliar to you. Stress starts to build. You enter the boss's office to be honest and open about some challenge you're encountering, expecting the same tender care received during orientation and your first few days. This time, however, things are way different. The boss, who came across as a pleasant, polite guy just a few weeks ago, becomes agitated and sarcastic. He even lets out a few jabs about your work ethic for good measure. Off you go into the wild blue yonder. A sense of devastation and dread overcomes you. Your confidence is rocked and your opinion about the cool vibe in the work environment has changed. These people were so nice during the interviews. The boss seemed so supportive and encouraging. What happened?

The focus of this chapter is on learning to be kind. People always mistake being nice versus being kind. I am sure that all the people at the office in the example above are "nice people," but once they are stressed, or once a demand they placed upon you does not finalize as requested, they suddenly cease to seem nice. You get hit with insults and a lot of negativity.

In fact, when you think about it, you'll realize there are people everywhere who "appear" nice on the surface. There are recurring news stories about the nice guy who tried to have his new wife murdered for her life insurance policy, or that salesman who seemed so nice before taking us for a ride for an extra thousand dollars—and we haven't even started on the politicians. Acting nice is all around us.

HOMAGE TO MY DAD: KILL 'EM WITH KINDNESS

Unfortunately, many of us fall for "niceness" because we want to believe the best about people. Such misjudgments have consequences.

Kindness and being nice are two very different behavioral traits. When we experience folks being *nice*, as opposed to being *kind*, there is a reason for their behavior. They want something from us. In some cases, they simply want us to like them; in other cases, they may want us to like a certain situation, usually for their secondary gain. For many "nice" people, the niceness is a way of validating their low self-esteem as they struggle to find a means to feel good about themselves in other ways. Sadly, this cycle can become utterly exhausting and self-destructive. They live their lives in search of new scenarios and opportunities in which they can be identified by others as "nice." These folks are not malicious, but stuck in a very unhealthy pattern of working extra hours or sticking around in that lopsided relationship. Why? Because nice people are liked. Everyone wants to be liked. In many cases, however, being liked is a trap. People who are pigeonholed as "nice," afraid of being perceived as not nice, will not stand up for themselves or share their true feelings with the world. This attitude leads to frustration or inner conflict that may, in turn, lead to unhealthy coping behaviors.

Our boss in the example above, and the other workers who grew frustrated with your work that day, were no longer nice. They finally showed their true colors. Their original "niceness" was a show, akin to a musical act or dramatic performance. You did not give them what they wanted, so being nice went out the door. Niceness at the office can be nothing more than the emotional manipulation of people whom it is important to please. How you behave when a new employee makes his first request or mistake is the proof of a far greater strength: being kind.

What many folks forget is that being kind is actually quite simple. Holding a door open for someone, letting a driver move into your lane, letting a stranger on the street know when she dropped something—these are all examples of kindness and courtesy. In all those cases, we ask for nothing in return. It feels good to assist another person.

Furthermore, kind people are not pushovers. They set limits and boundaries on others. They do not allow others to take advantage of them because they are not being "nice" to gain something. Because kind people love and value themselves, they are not concerned about whether their egos are fulfilled through others' endorsements of their niceness. As a result, they allow themselves more free space in their minds to be positive, creative, and successful.

Now, let's think back to that new boss who was nice during the interview phase and now is treating you with intense anger. How is it that his personality changed so quickly within a few weeks? He struggled with the inner conflict that inevitably comes with being merely "nice." Because you caused frustration in his life, he realized the tactic of being nice did not work this time. As a result, he tried a different strategy—being angry to non-verbally

HOMAGE TO MY DAD: KILL 'EM WITH KINDNESS

entice you to work harder and figure things out without direction.

Now it's up to you to respond. Instantly, you became angry with him for his snarky attitude. But since you are "kind" and not just "nice," you realize that, like so many "nice" people, he is probably hurting inside. His fragile ego was activated and, to cope with your situation, his only option was to show anger. Most folks like this are hurting a great deal inside. The boss might have immense difficulties at home with his spouse and his children. Possibly one of his parents is ill, and the emotions he is struggling with are manifested as being stern or gruff.

There is no reason to berate you in the office, as a method of inspiring you to improve your performance, after you've only been working there for two weeks. When you understand that and become mindful that most people manifest anger and the sudden loss of being nice because of their personal dilemmas, i.e., their desire to show their true feelings versus their desire to be universally liked, you can show kindness even in the midst of a personal attack. You can make the choice not to retaliate, but to listen and understand. As they say, "kill'em with kindness."

Psychiatry can be a very dangerous business. In the hospital inpatient units, patients with severe mental illness can become aggressive and violent on a whim. During my first year, a gentleman undergoing a severe manic episode became ruthlessly aggressive. I barely missed being on the receiving end of a right hook to the face as he tried to run from a mental health worker. Yet once he was calm and less agitated, I could be there for him as his physician as if nothing transpired. When it comes to the disorders which our patients struggle to overcome, our training calls for the utmost in understanding.

One particular night endures in my mind as the single worst clinical experience I have had—the experience in which I struggled the most to remain neutral and remain kind. Sarah was well known to us psychiatry residents. She suffered from severe cystic fibrosis, and her likelihood of ever seeing her eighteenth birthday was not high. Fourteen years old when I started my residency, she was in and out of the psychiatry inpatient unit for kids over and over again for her severe behavioral disorder and frequent bouts of aggression. Her defiance had an extra element beyond the standard oppositional behavior: she also refused to cooperate with the daily difficult behavioral and medication regimen that kids with cystic fibrosis must comply with to remain medically stable. We residents were aware on multiple admissions that she required a transfer to the medical floor because she developed a cough or showed signs of infections that required more intensive medical care than we could provide in the psychiatric unit.

Over time, the residents became jaded about Sarah. This behavior was just her norm. On many occasions, we lost sight of her frustration regarding her repeated transfers between hospitals. She wanted to be a normal, everyday teenager, but unfortunately her medical illness did not allow it.

One busy brisk night in late fall, I was on call and running near empty—I had been in the hospital for seventeen hours—when my pager beeped. It was the nurse from the child inpatient unit, answering my return call and informing me I needed to come medically evaluate Sarah. Her temperature had spiked, meaning that, once again, she needed to be transferred to the medical hospital. Tired and acting instinctively, with my frustration tolerance level running low, I walked quickly to the unit. As I approached, I could already hear yelling.

I walked inside. There was Sarah, pacing the floor. She knew what her elevated temperature meant, and wasn't happy: she just wanted to go to bed and be reassessed in the morning. Unfortunately, hospital policy stated that she required the transfer. Using the last of my empathy, I tried to calm her down by explaining that she had experienced this situation before and knew the drill; I was asking her to simply be quiet and allow me to get through this transfer so I could go to bed.

Sarah didn't let up. As I called the ambulance to assist in her transfer and eventually called her mother to inform her of what was happening, Sarah became more agitated. In that moment, I did not stop to appreciate that this poor early-adolescent girl just wanted to be a normal kid. I lost sight of the person in front of me, who had so little control over her surroundings and whose life was dictated by temperatures and coughs.

At some point, Sarah walked away. Then came an experience that would forever give me a deeper understanding of the emotional challenges of being a mental health practitioner. As I focused on my paperwork, it was quiet and completely dark except for the light coming from the computer monitor. A short time passed.

A spidey-sense came over me. Something did not feel right.

Instinctively, without thought and in a millisecond, I whirled my chair around and back. Sarah had come up from behind me with a janitor's flashlight—easily a ten-pound workman's tool. Now she had it raised up over her head with both hands, about to unleash her fury onto my skull. I rolled back; she swung, missed, and fell over. The clatter prompted the nursing and mental health staff to run over, grab her, and walk her to the isolation room until the ambulance arrived.

I was startled and disconcerted. I still think about what would have happened if my skull had taken the full impact of that heavy steel flashlight. A bleeding brain or a skull fracture could have been the worst-case outcome. As it turned out, however, Sarah was transferred and the night ended without further incident. My residency training continued; life went on. I treated Sarah on other occasions. Three years later, while completing my child psychiatry fellowship, I heard that she had passed.

HOMAGE TO MY DAD: KILL 'EM WITH KINDNESS

I tell this story here because meeting Sarah, and witnessing her distress, advanced my understanding of how to be kind. On the night of the flashlight incident, I failed in providing the much-needed empathy for Sarah that could have decreased her desire to inflict severe harm on me. Her behavior was not hard to explain: she was in intense pain. Emotionally, I can only imagine the difficulty of living a majority of her life being shuttled back and forth between psychiatric and medical hospitals. What child asks for that?

Becoming a psychiatrist, and having the honor to work with patients like Sarah, allowed me to grow as a psychiatrist. She taught me to look past the aggressive act—to look past the attacks (physical and otherwise) that people may instigate because they are frustrated with the treatment options or prognoses that I have given them. I have learned to be patient. I have learned to be kinder to those who are dealing with loss, rejection, illness, and despair.

When people lose control over parts of their lives, it's not unnatural for them to display negative emotions. On a more personal level, how many times have you become angry with a parent who is aging because he is maybe more forgetful, or asks the same question multiple times over? How we as people respond to people who are hurting is a representation of how kind we can be to our fellow man and woman. We can do something more powerful and worthy than retaliating or becoming defensive.

Our personal journeys to be kind start in our home lives. The social modeling of parents for their children remains, in my opinion, the greatest predictor of their children's eventual tendency to be kind as adults. Regardless of social status or wealth, our adult behaviors towards others in sight of our children will teach them the right—or wrong—means to cope with frustration and stressors. If your child sees you become agitated when someone cuts you off in the car, when a worker at the store does not provide you with adequate service, or when you are settling a relationship conflict with your spouse, you are modeling such behavior for your child. For better or worse, the child, in turn, will use such behavior as the roadmap for treating others when stressed.

I think back to our boss in the example in the beginning of the chapter. I wonder how his parents behaved when he did not perform to their standards. It's very possible that their initial niceness gave way to agitation when they became frustrated at their child's behavior and tried to teach their child a lesson. Most likely that did not work, but what they did do successfully was show their child that, when you are not content with another person's behavior, you berate that person and become agitated to make your point. Not a good strategy.

When I was six years old, my parents and I lived in Niagara Falls, New York. Finances were a large source of stress for my parents. My mother worked at a supermarket as a cashier and my father was constantly between sales jobs, each trying to make ends meet. But you know what? I never would have known. Regardless of my behavior or grades, they maintained an atmosphere of emotional neutrality. They treated me well and never displaced their adult anxieties onto me.

We spent a brief three years in Niagara Falls. My most powerful childhood memory of my father was at this time in my life. A favorite pastime of ours, after school or on the weekends, was going to the Aquarium of Niagara, where the seal exhibit was visible from the outside. I loved watching these beautiful animals swim and play around with their peers. My father and I would visit at least once a week. I was spending quality time with my dad, away from the TV and exposed to the beauty of nature.

What actually is the most powerful moment from this story?

I have never actually been inside the Aquarium of Niagara.

I never realized, until I was in my twenties, that this was the truth. We didn't have the money for admission to the real aquarium. We always went to see the seals in their tank, which could be watched from outside the aquarium; we never entered the building. Within his financial limitations, my father showed me, his son, more about being kind, loving each other, and showing affection towards animals than any fancy present or extravagant European trip could provide. Our trips to the aquarium were consistently free of negative emotions, and full of being silly while looking at beautiful creatures of the sea.

As I have grown into a man and eventually a child psychiatrist, I have come to realize that we do not need wealth or fame to pass on this important gift to our children: modeling how to be kind. We just need to become part of their world, limit their exposure to the challenges of adulthood, and model for them how to love others and ourselves.

This chapter's goals are to maximize your capacity for kindness and to guide you towards becoming a role model for your peers and the less experienced people around you. As this chapter is the last in the book, I hope that you have witnessed some gains within yourself, such as becoming less negative, less angry, less anxious, and a more active listener; that you have let go of your ego a little and become closer with healthier peers; and that you have moved a little outside your comfort zone to enable yourself to grow. If you have managed to move forward with any of these, guess what? I bet you are already a little kinder!

Let's go a little further. As always, the work begins with you. If you were the boss in the opening example, perhaps you can identify some of his own issues that are giving rise to his difficult interactions with people. He uses negative language, his ego appears fractured, he becomes angry, and he certainly is not being kind. If he were to come to my office, how would I begin?

HOMAGE TO MY DAD: KILL 'EM WITH KINDNESS

As an initial matter, we have to learn to become kind to ourselves. It's likely that the stress of the office is affecting him. Why? Does he exercise and have a good diet? That is always my first question. If not, it is possible he does not have a healthier outlet to release his pent-up anger, so that he uses work and staff beneath him to displace his anger.

Does he diversify his life and maintain a healthy curiosity about interests outside of work? If not, is it possible that too much of his emotions are connected to the job—so much so, in fact, that when you (the new hire) came in without meeting his expectations, his ego was fractured and he felt he needed to unleash his fury onto you to feel good?

Lastly, is his relationship functioning well, and are he and his spouse communicating well? Using negative language at home, with the further accumulation of negativity that results, leads to fewer acts of kindness. I want you to think all of these things for yourself. Practice noticing when you feel the urge to be unkind to another. Is this because you are hurting inside? Remember, if you feel terrible yourself, you probably will act terrible towards others. Learn to let it go. Learn to forgive others' weaknesses. Use the chapters in the book to improve your interactions with others and your environment.

Here are some specific ideas to be kind.

- You are sitting on the bus or subway and an elderly person or pregnant woman comes down the aisle. Make eye contact with the other person and offer your seat. He or she may not take it, but it is kind to ask.
- You are walking down a busy street in your city or town and you recognize someone who appears a little lost. Walk over and ask, "Are you looking for a specific place or street?" Guiding someone to the right locations feels quite good, as many of us can remember being confused by foreign streets in other cities.
- Recognize when leaving the post office that someone is carrying a few boxes and hold the door. Not every person will say thank you—but again, this is for you, not for them. You know you performed a kind gesture.
- You are walking towards your car and you see someone driving down the street slowly looking for a spot. Getting his attention and letting him know you are walking towards your car to leave relieves the stress of looking for a parking spot.
- Everyone on Facebook always tries to post his or her achievements. Unfortunately, for many, real life gets in the way and tragedy can strike. When friends undergo traumatic experiences, sending a direct message—or, even more, calling them to see how they are doing and listening, will help them get through their day.
- The neighbor next door is getting older. Offer to mow the lawn or shovel the driveway for this neighbor.

HOMAGE TO MY DAD: KILL 'EM WITH KINDNESS

    Preventing those around you from possibly hurting themselves is quite altruistic.
- Your sibling has been under stress at work and would love to get away, but has no one to watch a beloved pet. Volunteering to watch the pet would be so appreciated.

The list can go on and on, and I am sure that as you read this list, you probably can come up with your own ideas. I understand that, in the beginning, some of these behaviors may feel unusual for you, such as interacting with strangers and putting yourself out there, but I ask you to make the attempt. The health benefits are massive—not just emotionally, but also biologically (showing kindness has been linked to better cardiovascular health). Just like training for a sport or preparing to run for a marathon, the more you practice, the better you will get. And as a reminder: just like practicing an instrument, or working in therapy, you guys need to go out there and give it a shot!

TAKEAWAY POINTS

- Being kind and being nice are two different processes. Kindness asks for nothing in return and allows for setting limits.

- Always being the "nice" person can lead to burnout, anxiety, and depression.

- When someone is not being kind to you, you have a choice in terms of how to respond. Remember, it takes two to tango—or to begin an argument.

- When you notice yourself being "unkind," your behavior may be a sign of frustration in other aspects of life, i.e. work, relationships, family. You may need to find a healthy outlet for your frustration.

- Practicing kindness is like a skill. With practice, it comes naturally and feels good!

AFTERWORD

Life has so many finish lines. At the beginning of every meeting, date, or trip, we always have our expectations of how something will end. We need the right tools to ensure, with our best sense of empowerment, that we have the best outcome.

When I ran the New York City marathon, I used all the tools presented to make it as pleasant as possible. I still faced strong adversity. Simply going to therapy or seeking mental health treatment does not end adversity. We as therapists hope to guide you better on your journey as you face adversity in your life. We offer tools and guidance so you become more aware and mindful as you make decisions in life.

I hope that based on the shared tools in this book and my stories, you are inspired to take on your version of the marathon, no matter how big or small. Just remember that going for the 26.2-mile race right off the bat is extremely difficult. Start small. Prepare yourself for life's version of a 5K and gradually improve. Learning and practicing new skills will increase your endurance and tolerance in the face of life's challenges.

Some days we will not be able to finish that race. That's okay. Life's greatest moments appear when we learn from our experiences and can alter an aspect of who we are to ensure that, next time, there may be a better outcome. As with therapy, I applaud anyone who picks up this book and tries to add new skills to his or her life. It's brave to want to work on oneself consciously.

I hope this book helps you in your journey. I look forward to seeing you on the track of life!

ABOUT THE AUTHOR

Johnny Lops, D.O., received his medical degree from the Philadelphia College of Osteopathic Medicine. He completed his adult psychiatry residency training, and a fellowship in child and adolescent psychiatry, at the Hofstra North Shore-Long Island Jewish School of Medicine. The team psychiatrist for the Brooklyn Nets from 2012 to 2015, he is currently a clinical instructor of psychiatry for the Maimonides Medical Center Psychiatry Residency Program and an assistant professor of psychiatry at the New York College of Osteopathic Medicine.

An accomplished actor and film producer, Lops has starred in numerous stage productions and television commercials. He lives in Brooklyn with his wife.

www.ingramcontent.com/pod-product-compliance
Lightning Source LLC
Chambersburg PA
CBHW032036290426
44110CB00012B/821